Women at the Wheel

42 Stories of Freedom, Fanbelts and the Lure of the Open Road

Marilyn Root

Sourcebooks, Inc.
Naperville, IL

Published by Sourcebooks, Inc.
P.O. Box 372
Naperville, IL 60566
630-961-3900
Fax: 630-961-2168

Library of Congress Cataloging-in-Publication Data

Root, Marilyn.
    Women at the wheel: 42 stories of freedom, fanbelts and the lure of the open road / photographs and text by Marilyn Root.
        p.   cm.
    ISBN 1-57071-443-6 (alk. paper)
    1. Automobiles—Popular works. 2. Women automobile drivers—Pictorial works. I. Title.
    TL146.5.R66 1999
    796.7'082—dc21   99-12636
                                                                                          CIP

Printed and bound in the United States of America
10 9 8 7 6 5 4 3 2 1

To the memory of my mother Jean, who, much to my surprise,
eventually let me drive her maroon Valiant to the mall.

Acknowledgments

There is a long list of people without whom *Women At the Wheel* would not have been possible.

Firstly, I would like to extend my thanks to all the wonderful women who have shared their lives and stories with me. Secondly, I offer apologies to the many women I photographed and interviewed whose stories, due to space constraints, could not be included.

I would also like to thank Roberta LaBarbera and Dana Carpenter, Gina Catanzarite, Lucille Treganowan, Karen Kahn, Judith Vincent, Miriam Goodman, and Nancy Hazard. Cal Kolbe and Steve Nossiter both listened, offering ideas and support.

Jennifer McKay, Susanne Theis, and everyone at the Orange Show Foundation deserve particular thanks for welcoming me into their automotive family.

Harrod Blank, art car king, graciously led me down the road to the art cars.

Armor and Ron Keller, Beverly Hayes and Brian Howard, Alice Evergreen, Janice Cardoza and Pat Shearman, Bill Stevenson, and Diane Afes are among those who have offered warm hospitality along the highway. Becky Sargent and Tom Jones provided hospitality as well as excellent compilation tapes for road trips. Howard Zaharoff provided expertise and an all important sense of humor. Lys Guillorn contributed expertise and enthusiasm. Of course, I would also like to thank Deb Werksman for her expertise, enthusiasm, editing, and her ability to blend the stories into a book.

Table of Contents

Introduction

It seems as if I've always been surrounded by automobiles. From the time I attended my first vintage car show as a toddler, too young to appreciate the luxurious Packards on display, and the time I climbed into the back seat of my mother's red and white 1955 Willys a few years later, I was fascinated with cars; first, with their shapes and sounds, and eventually with the independence they offered.

My own Datsun 210 was a "practical" car, and lived to reach 138,000 miles in fourteen years. Its only bit of rust resulted from a romantic evening when it was parked on a San Francisco hill. The emergency brake was nudged off during a parting kiss, and my Datsun briefly met the pointy nose of a Cadillac parked directly behind it. Whenever I caught sight of its tiny dent, and the resulting rust, I was lulled back to fond memories of that evening.

The Datsun survived the heat waves of Southern California summers, the snow of Massachusetts, the trials and tribulations of city combat driving, and was even once stolen and recovered. It never complained and never left me stranded. Its life was cut short when another car plowed into the driver's side. When its door was pried open, I saw that the Datsun had given its life for mine. Its frame was bent, yet its deluxe blue pinstriping held on, and I was fine. Even though the Datsun didn't make 200,000 miles, as I was once certain it would, it protected me beyond my wildest dreams, and will never be forgotten.

Today I drive a Saturn, unassuming on the outside, adorned on the interior with mementos of the road trips I love to take.

In my professional life, I am a photographer of events, places, and people. While photographing one woman with a very important feline friend for a book project, I realized that our relationships are not only with people or animals, but also with our possessions. Among our most treasured possessions, our cars loom large, helping us, as they do, to live our lives to the fullest.

Women and cars, I thought. Why not? Even automotive advertisements from the 1920s featured women prominently in the driver's seat. Today, women buy almost half of the cars sold in the United States—roughly eight million new cars and another eight million used cars each year. The automotive object of affection doesn't have to be expensive, classic, or fancy. During the course of photographing women for this book, I realized just how special each and every vehicle is to its owner.

Over a five-year period, I photographed and interviewed nearly one hundred women for this book. When I talked with women about their cars, motorcycles, trucks, and buses, I heard more than simple stories about practical transportation. They shared with me their tales of independence, growth, creativity, growing up, growing older, children, relationships, divorce, and loss. Our conversations were filled with laughter too, as we recounted our automotive histories, the trials and tribulations of driving, the nicknames we bestowed on our cars, our urges to personalize and decorate them, popular culture, the lure of the road, and the innumerable ways our vehicles change our lives. Indeed, for many women the stories of their relationships with their vehicles are not only those of transportation, but of transformation.

The forty-two women in this book express their automotive affection with choices ranging from the Stanley Steamer (marketed to women in the early part of the twentieth century because it was easier to start than a car with a crank) to a late-model Saturn, and everything in between. In these pages, you'll find women who are competent, creative, compassionate, and passionate, with their vehicles: cars, buses, trucks, vans, motorcycles; factory-equipped, or personally embellished; classics from the 1960s or shiny, brand-new models straight from the dealer's showroom.

As much as possible, I use each woman's own words to relate her own story. Many of these women have become adept at car repairs; some have turned their know-how into careers. Others travel thousands of miles in our great country and beyond, seeing the sights and enjoying the freedom. The women in this book often relate to their vehicles as a part of themselves.

One thing is certain: women at the wheel are a force to be reckoned with, steering their lives toward new horizons.

Marilyn Root, Massachusetts, January 1999

Sometimes, you just have to do something out of the ordinary…

Serena Watson keeps her 1955 T-Bird's hardtop in storage. She asserts, "I only drive it on days like today, beautiful autumn days, and on summer weekends on Cape Cod." After all, if you owned one of the first three hundred 1955 T-Bird convertibles, like this black beauty, you'd baby it as much as possible.

"I don't want to put too many miles on it. The car is forty years old, and it'll only have 40,000 miles, so that's not bad." You get the feeling Serena is trying to convince herself.

"I bought the T-Bird during the summer that my father was dying," Serena recounts, "I was running around looking for things to make him comfortable. As I was driving around the rotary, out of the corner of my eye I saw its little lights in a dusty garage. I did a U-turn and said to myself, 'That's the one.'"

Serena's father, who died about three weeks later, "would have loved the car. He was a test pilot, he loved engines, and he loved to drive. He's driving up there right now."

For at least six months, Serena had coveted a specific kind of Thunderbird. "I thought it would be fun just to have that small Thunderbird, not the big one that came out later, but the real little one." Looking through the want-ads was frustrating. She admits, "I didn't realize they were so expensive."

Of course, once Serena put away the want-ads, she spotted this car. "It was in an auto body garage, all dusty, but I knew then it was one of the first, small T-Birds, and it had a 'FOR SALE' sign propped on its hood." Acting on impulse, Serena says, "I just thought 'What the heck, let's give it a whirl!' It was so beautiful; and it was just the right size."

An estate sale car, Serena admits her T-Bird was expensive. "But I thought 'I could be dead tomorrow.' It seemed like a great deal of money at the time, so I just broke it up into months, a little here, and a little there. I said to myself, 'I think I'll just blow it, and do something uncharacteristic,' which is what you have to do sometimes when you're forty-four years old. You just have to do something out of the ordinary."

This T-Bird is indeed extraordinary. "The guy who owned it took every nut and bolt apart and put the whole thing back together; it's like a brand-new car. I thought maybe I'd tinker around with it, maybe change it's oil." Serena confides, "Even though I never thought I had it in me, I'm becoming more mechanical." Serena knows she could sell her T-Bird tomorrow; it's never going to go down in value. But she intends to keep it: "I picture my thirteen-year-old daughter driving away from her wedding in this car."

Serena joined a car club "to share the obsession. There wasn't another woman at the car show, so I do stand out a little. I want to learn about this car, even though there's nothing luxurious about it. It's all manual, and that's the way it should be. Compared with newer cars, the engine looks almost like a lawnmower engine.

"In the T-Bird, you can really see more, and you notice more when the top is down. You're much more aware of your surroundings.

"I'll never regret buying the T-Bird. I'm trying to come out of myself a little bit, be a little more aggressive, and a little more open. I'm trying to change my personality. This car is the way I do it! After all, why should the men have all the fun?"

Serena Watson from Massachusetts with her 1955 Thunderbird convertible
(one of the first three hundred 1955 T-Bird convertibles).

The only thing I regret is that I didn't decorate my car sooner…

Ever since she can remember, Rebecca Boren dreamed of driving a toy-covered car. "When I was little I always thought it would be fun to stick things onto my car, even though I'd never seen other decorated cars."

Rebecca's work as a physician's assistant in neurosurgery is reflected in her vehicle. "There's a spinal cord, and a vertebral column on the back of my car, and a glow-in-the-dark femur, but there aren't any brains. I had some latex brains, but they were rubber, and I'm still trying to figure out how to get rubber things to stick to the car. So far, they peel right off.

"One of my friends was weaning her child so she gave me little plastic nipples. I placed them carefully over the squirters for the windshield, so when you squirt the windshield wipers, you're looking at the nipples!

"I don't know exactly how many toys are on my car, maybe a hundred or more, but I've got a mailbox on the roof, for people to leave me notes and toys." Rebecca runs through a list of the toys on her car.

"There's a Jack-in-the-box, a Medusa, little bendy toys, road signs, globes, wagons, gum ball machines, and a giant molar my husband wants to solder a filling into.

"There's also a knight in shining armor, kitties, slugs, and ferrets; a bottle of spilled nail polish, a woman in a bathtub, and plastic cockroaches heading towards chocolate chip muffins. The cockroaches were being chased by a can of Raid, but someone stole the Raid! There's also an Oscar Mayer Wiener car, a tiny lava lamp, trolls, hula girls, monkeys and gargoyles, eyeballs and skeletons, snakes, fish, footsteps, a little train set, and a poison dart frog. There are giant flies, miniature teakettles, a little Cuisinart, rubber duckies, horses and pigs, judges and gavels, a slot machine, mushrooms, and an oven. There are monster women, and a rubber chicken, a tarantula, a bat girl, some melted ice cream, a skatefish, a cobra squirt gun, a nose, a little phone, a mouse in a trap, a camera and a fossil, a fortune cookie, handcuffs, a hot dog, and a magic wand.

"For many years I drove an old Honda Prelude. I had toys by the bagful collected, and I was ready to do up my car, but nobody thought it was a good idea. Everyone thought I was completely insane, and they promised me I would regret it. I can't believe I let them convince me. Finally, I just decided to ignore them and decorate my new car!"

At first, Rebecca decided to concentrate on painting the exterior. "I wanted to keep the red, but add some splatter painting. I'm very technical, so I called up a long list of auto body shops. I explained that I wanted to splatter-paint the car, and asked them how to go about it. Ninety percent of the places assured me they would *never* want to, and couldn't understand why I would. I wanted everything done right, because I wanted to make sure the splatter painting would last.

"Finally, I found a body shop that would accommodate me. After collecting all my information, I came in at seven o'clock in the morning, armed with fine sandpaper. I sanded down the whole car, which was really scary, because it looked all dull; flat and pink, which is kind of nasty for a red car. I was really scared, wondering if my car would ever look good again. But I had faith in these people. They let me work at the shop, because after I got through painting, they would "clear coat" the car, which is what gives it that glossy luster, and protects the color from fading. I had to do a million other things before I was ready to paint. There were all these substances to remove the dust, and I had to move this high powered air hose all over the car. Finally, I brought the car into a completely dust free booth, and splattered it with paint. By that time it was already six o'clock in the evening." Five layers of professionally applied clear coating provided the finishing touch, and Rebecca's car was "done."

But something was missing. "I drove around for several months with my splatter-painted car, but it just wasn't enough. It was subtly pretty, but you had to be standing close to the car, and it had to be light to really see it. It didn't do enough for me.

"I have the taste of a child, and I'd collected lots of little amusing, colorful, eye-catching items, but it was several months before I did the first batch of gluing. When I met my husband, Doug, I knew he was 'the one' because when I told him my decision to glue all the toys to my car, he said, 'Oh great, it'll be so much fun!' instead of the 'Oh no!' I got from other people."

Driving around with all these toys is one thing, but keeping the toys attached isn't always easy. "I had all these great little things, but I parked in this evil, vile neighborhood, right near a school. One night, school kids walking by just absolutely savaged it. I was in tears because 50 percent of the toys were gone. They must have put their gnarly little feet against the car and really pulled, because these toys were attached with silicone and sub-flooring adhesive, which is really hard to tear apart. I can deal with it, once in a while, when I come outside, and something's missing from the car, and I think, 'Oh well, some kid took it home because they couldn't live without it,' but this was just savage vandalism. They didn't even take pleasure out of keeping the toys; they just littered the street with them. These evil little children tore the head off of Jabba the Hut while he was sitting on the front of my car. One of my neighbors found him in the gutter, but he was missing an arm, so I gave him a blender for an arm, to fight off any other little evil kids, and rewarded him with a crown for going through this terrible ordeal."

In spite of the initial discouragement, Rebecca finds most people reacting to her car with smiles and laughter. "Once, I was double-parked and I saw a policeman standing by my car, so I ran out and told him I'd move it, and he said, 'No don't move it; I'm enjoying looking at it, and it's fabulous.' He could have given me a ticket and scolded me, but he loved it. And just today a policeman pulled me over. I didn't think I was speeding, but he asked only one question, 'Why?' and smiled. I answered 'Why not?'

"I'm really shocked at how many people say it's beautiful. I don't know whether it's beautiful, but it's fun; it's me and I love it. It's my soul on metal. The only thing I regret is that I didn't decorate my car sooner."

Rebecca Boren from Massachusetts with her 1992 Honda, "Meowwwmobile,"
named for her four indoor cats: two Persians, one Bengal, and a Longhair Tortoiseshell.

There must be angels protecting us on the road…

Seventeen-year-old Emily Burkes-Nossiter and her mother Betty Burkes agree there must be angels protecting them on the road. Betty feels certain that angels protect her, because she claims never to have had an accident in the decades since she learned to drive in her mother's 1954 Chevrolet.

Betty loves speed, and the feeling of invincibility driving brings, but she's aware it only takes a second for something to go wrong. "I have been in situations where there's no reason I shouldn't have had an accident. I'm a good driver, and I'm careful, but I do all the things that people who have accidents do. I take my eyes off the road. Sometimes I've stopped just in the nick of time."

Emily had two car accidents within a few weeks of each other. On her way to a party, driving on a Cape Cod road known as 'suicide alley,' Emily was in the middle of a four-car collision involving three Saabs and a Bronco. Emily, uninjured in the totaled Toyota and protected by "road angels" now admits to "Saab-phobia."

Not long afterwards, driving on a snowy oceanfront road, Emily experienced her second mishap. "I

turned a corner, and hit a patch of ice. All of a sudden I had no control, and went up on an embankment. I guess the front end of the car kind of hit a tree. It was scarier than the first accident, sitting in this hunk of metal." Once again, Emily was fine. So this was the second and final accident, right?

Betty interjects, "What about the third accident?" Emily interrupts: "Two accidents!" Betty says, "Oh, you *did* bump that car, and you didn't even know you'd bumped it!" Emily responds, "Mom, it wasn't a car, it was a tree, and it was a *little* dent!" Betty discusses her daughter's driving, "She just didn't pay the kind of attention she needed to." Emily admits, "When I first started driving, I wasn't all that attentive. I wasn't scared, and maybe I should have been. A lot of times I had ten thousand things going on in my head. The accidents really taught me to pay attention!"

Betty Burkes and Emily Burkes-Nossiter from Massachusetts with their 1989 Toyota wagon.

Why shouldn't your car be a work of art?

You could be excused for confusing Lynn Finley's home with her 1970 Volkswagen van; especially since she has been known to keep part of her living room set inside the van, and both are filled with leopard print.

Says Lynn, "My living room walls are covered with leopard print sheets, and the furniture is overstuffed, 1970s brown fur, the television is draped with a leopard shawl, and I've covered the Aladdin's lamps with pieces of fake leopard fur; they're very tasteful.

"The van was a present I bought for myself two-and-a-half years ago to celebrate my sobriety. I've always wanted a Volkswagen, especially a Beetle. I work as a massage therapist and sometimes need to carry a table and a lot of stuff. This van is big enough to carry almost my entire house."

This standard 1970 Volkswagen van endured a lengthy rehabilitation process. "I think it had 135,000 miles on it, but I'm not sure, because the odometer doesn't roll over to the hundreds. Originally it was off-white, with holes all around it's windshield. The rain came in, and it was very cold since the heater didn't work, but I saw its promise. I had the body work done first, and then it was painted. I put about $8,000 into it, which, for a vehicle you *love*, and that has a newly rebuilt engine in it, is not *that* bad. Now her name is 'Gus' or 'Gussie' as in, 'Hop on the bus, Gus,' or 'All gussied up.' She's also known as 'Cat Van Deux.' Now she purrs, and of course, she's definitely a female.

"The first part of Gussie's cosmetic rehabilitation was the flesh-colored base paint, and then a friend airbrushed the orange parts, and I sponge painted with black automotive paint to make the leopard spots, and the finishing touch was a layer of protective clear coat. Once I saw how well it came out, I had to start getting the inside ready. First I did the seat covers, and went on from there." Today, towels, sheets, rugs, and pillows with varying spots and stripes make most of the surfaces part of a mobile jungle experience.

Lynn's van acts as a barometer, showing her the tolerance people have for difference. "Usually, the bus elicits a positive response. People are always pointing, and nudging the person next to them, then they turn around and wave. Sometimes I see people who look hostile though, and I figure, those are people who just don't like life in general. It's as if you're parading on their rain. They just don't *want* to be happy! Your car is probably the second most expensive purchase you ever make in your life, and why shouldn't it be something you really like—a work of art? So I enjoy it. It makes me happy, and every time I see it, I smile. My younger son, who is twenty-one, loves the bus; he likes my weirdness. My older son is more conservative.

"As you drive down the street, other Volkswagen owners wave at you. It's like being a member of a club. Volkswagens are such a commitment, once you own one, you're committed to keeping it up. A certain personality owns a Volkswagen van or Beetle; you're almost kindred spirits. I drive it every day, and it's like having a parade every day of your life. I see men smile at it, and I know they're remembering their college days."

Growing up, Lynn never imagined owning a vehicle like Gussie. "My first car was a 1955 Chevy when I was a senior in high school, circa 1965. All I wanted back then was to marry some nice guy, and have 2.2 kids, live in a vine-covered cottage, and attend tap-dance lessons for the daughter I was going to have, and PTA and Cub Scouts meetings. I got the two kids, the marriage part didn't work, and I'm not good at PTA. I just wasn't cut out for that. Now I take tap-dancing. I used to be afraid to try new things, and then I hopped in this vehicle, and it was about a week later I realized; wow, driving way up high in a van is fun!

"We can celebrate uniqueness, and enjoy being different. Anybody can be the same as everybody else. I love the leopard patterns, and the fabric comes in all different colors. Leopard is a way of life!"

Lynn Finley from Texas with her 1970 Volkwagen van, "Cat Van Deux," aka "Gus" or "Gussie."

She represents liberation to me…

The traditional graduation gift in Deb Ellstrom's family was always an automobile. There was only one hitch. "Before I ever got a car, my father bought my brothers a pair of VW Beetles for a total of $50. He told them, 'Here are your first cars, now you're going to learn to repair them.' Those cars basically weren't even in running shape, so my brothers learned about mechanics by pulling the cars apart with my father's help and supervision."

Deb's father didn't treat her differently than her brothers, though Deb uses a wheelchair, and drives using hand controls. "When it was my turn, Dad bought a 1966 Dodge Polara from a friend whose wife had wrapped it around a telephone pole. Its front end was completely done in, and it sustained some minor damage on the passenger side, so he bought it for $50, saying, 'Here is your learning experience; if you want to drive this car, it's up to you to fix it. I will help you, and you will do most of the work.'

"So I learned to work on this big, hulking Polara, with its 383 V-8 engine with single barrel carburetor. We straightened its frame, pulled the dents out of the doors, and the entire nose off the car, and I was on the frozen ground in March hammering the dents out. Since the Polara was white, and almost as long as my uncle's Cadillac, "Ely the White Elephant" was a perfect name. Ely lasted six years until someone made a left turn into me. He didn't signal, he was drunk, he veered right into my path, pushed the engine in, and did all sorts of damage. Still, it lasted six more months."

Then Deb began her twelve-year relationship with "Scamper," otherwise known as a Plymouth Scamp. "In 1982, I decided to drive from Massachusetts to Tucson, Arizona, to attend graduate school in biology. I had never been further than the New York State line, and my sister came along for the ride. By the time we reached Connecticut, the car was overheating, but I was determined it was a minor problem.

"I put in a new thermostat, filled the tank, and drove. It was fine when we reached Indianapolis, so we decided to drive all night long until Texas. As we reached New Mexico, I realized the alternator wasn't working and found an auto parts shop. By this time it was noon, and hot! I was standing there with my tools out, with my arms grimy to the elbows pulling out the old alternator and putting in the new one. It only took about twenty minutes. The parts shop guy kept asking whether he could call AAA for us, and I was able to answer, 'No thanks, we've got it fixed.' They were standing there shaking their heads. I had the tools; I knew how to diagnose it and make sure it was running properly.

"It is such a satisfying feeling to diagnose something, and be able to get in there and fix it, and know that you did it right, and you didn't need someone else to go and do it. There's a sense of accomplishment you don't get when you just drive your car to be repaired and tell them to fix whatever needs fixing."

Eventually, Deb relinquished the Scamp, then drove a Diplomat she named the "Anti-Chrysler" because "it had one problem after another."

Deb persevered in looking for the car of her dreams. "The Anti-Chrysler died on its way to meet the LeBaron. The listing said '1986 LeBaron in excellent shape; must sell, with power steering and brakes.' As I got out to look at the LeBaron, the Anti-Chrysler's head gasket went; there was water pouring out of its engine! On a cold, snowy morning, I sat and watched them tow it away, nodding and smiling. I hoped the demon left with it, because it had given me so much grief."

The LeBaron passed Deb's tests. "It's got lots of pick-up, especially for a four-cylinder engine, it handles nicely, there's good suspension, and the power is there when you need it. The transmission seems to shift up perfectly." For $950, Deb bought the LeBaron, with its newly rebuilt engine. "The interior is perfect; I can get my wheelchair in and out, and I should be able to do the maintenance work on its four-cylinder 2.2 liter engine."

Deb is ecstatic about her LeBaron. Her first big journey was to a successful job interview. "On the way back, I was cruising, thinking how wonderful it is to drive again. I didn't even care that I was on the freeway at 4:30 P.M. in rush hour traffic, because having a car is so integral to my feeling of independence.

"Eventually I knew I would name my new car. I began wondering about this LeBaron's name, going back over all the possibilities. Since it says LeBaron on the glove compartment, I start thinking of 'L' names, and realize that "Libby" works not only as "Libby LeBaron," but because she represents liberation for me. I depend on the car so much more, because I can't depend on buses, trains, or commuter rail services. Libby is really my liberation, she's my wheels, she gets me around every place I want to go, and I love to drive."

Deb Ellstrom from Massachusetts with her 1986 Chrysler LeBaron, "Libby."

When I left my husband I said to myself, I am going to get a convertible…

"I drove past it four times before I stopped," says Joan Daskey. "It's a 1983 LeBaron convertible. I was always looking for a convertible. I was married for twenty years, and I've been divorced for twenty years. A long time ago, when my husband Bill and I were together, we had a black convertible, an Oldsmobile, and I always remember taking the four kids to the beach, driving that convertible every day we could.

"When I left my husband I said to myself, 'I don't care if it's an old rattletrap, I'm going to have a convertible.' When I saw this one in Vermont last year it had just been shined up and it looked real nice. The top was down, and I fell in love as soon as I saw it. But I drove past it four times before I stopped. Each time I got more and more determined. Finally, I stopped the car and went right over to look. I was getting all undone in my dress, on my hands and knees to look underneath it."

Sixty-two-year-old Joan knew exactly what she wanted. "The seller wanted $1,400 for it, but I said, 'I'll give you $850 cash for it,' and he said, 'Great, sold!' Its book value is $3,000.

"Everyone warned me that it would be a money pit, and a gas-guzzler. I haven't had any trouble with it at all. It gets thirty miles to the gallon. My grown children warned me that a convertible would be dangerous, and I told them that if I die, at least I'll have a smile on my face. I've still got a good deal, that's what I think!"

Joan Daskey from Maine with her 1983 Chrysler LeBaron convertible.

When it's just you and your car out on the highway, you can think about anything…

Living in Bowling Green, Kentucky, the site of the National Corvette Museum, means Velma Koostras and her family are never far from exquisite examples of some of the world's most admired cars.

"I was content with driving a Cadillac. My husband owned a 1963 Corvette in college, and then he began working for a company that furnished a car. He sold his beloved Corvette, but he never recovered. My husband and two college-aged boys finally convinced me to see the purchase of a used Corvette as an investment. At first I thought, 'Here I am, a forty-five-year-old Mom, and I don't need a sporty Corvette!'"

Today, Velma drives the Corvette she and her husband bought, but she refers to it lovingly as "my car." She adds, "Now my husband drives a pickup truck." As for the Corvette, Velma says, "It's just like you're a whole different person when you're in the Corvette.

"When you drive a Bronco to the market, they put your groceries in the car, slam the trunk, and you leave. You drive the Cadillac, and you're a 'ma'am.' You drive to the grocery store in the Corvette and all

of a sudden everyone is talkative and friendly. Not that I'm a big flirt or anything, but it's fun to drive around; you certainly do get a few more looks than when you drive a family car."

Getting accustomed to driving the Corvette meant hitting the bridge joints a bit rougher. "You just have to get used to its wide wheels. Turning is a lot different, you can't just feel it the way you can in other cars. Believe it or not, it's terrible to parallel park, because the wheel is so wide it doesn't cut well. It's not like parking anything else, and it's a little rougher out on the highway." To make up for what might otherwise sound like complaints, Velma praises its features. "When you step on the gas, you don't have any problem passing cars; it's really fun to drive. I haven't gotten any tickets; I'm just lucky I guess."

Another advantage is the car's radio. "The faster you drive, to make up for road noise, the radio adjusts itself and becomes louder. You just drive down the highway cruising about 75 or 80 miles per hour and you've got this good music, and when you slow down, the radio goes down automatically.

"When it's just you and your car out on the highway, you can think about anything, and you can talk to yourself or sing and nobody will ever hear you."

As president-elect of the statewide Extension Homemakers, Velma will be driving her Corvette all over Kentucky, teaching new home management ideas. And when Velma's not cruising down the highway, she answers visitors' questions at her job at the National Corvette Museum. Velma is perfectly content to be surrounded by Corvettes and their enthusiastic owners on a daily basis.

Velma Koostras from Kentucky with her 1990 Corvette.

In the beginning no one took me seriously…

Sixty-five-year-old Lucille Treganowan never intended to make automobile transmissions her life's work. She dreamed of studying English in college, and teaching high school or college students. Today, this transmission expert's classroom is larger than that found on any campus, and she's more likely to be found under the hood of a car than lecturing from the podium.

Lucille's mission is to teach people of all ages about their cars, what to look for when buying a new or used vehicle, and how to take care of problems. She gathers her audience from living rooms across the nation as the host of the Home and Garden Television Network's "Lucille's Car Care Clinic," and has been aptly described as "America's Most Trusted Mechanic." She owns two "Transmissions by Lucille" shops.

Somewhere along the road, Lucille's life took an unexpected turn. "You never know where you're going to end up in life, and I had met and married a Pittsburgher while studying at the University of Arizona. So we moved to Pittsburgh, and the only thing I knew how to do was bookkeeping. Then I had three small children, and it looked like my husband and I weren't going to stay together, so I found a job in an auto repair shop doing clerical work, all the while attending the University of Pittsburgh. I *still* wanted to teach, but I got really fascinated with the work at the auto repair shop, and I never quite got it together to go back to school full-time, so I just learned the business!"

Lucille is so matter-of-fact, she makes it sound easy. "At first, I stuck to writing up customers' orders and doing the books, just as I was hired to do. But the customers always came to me with their questions. It was frustrating not to be able to answer them, so I began looking at the technical repair manuals.

"In the beginning, no one took me seriously. They'd say, 'Oh, go back to the office,' and that kind of thing.

"The turning point arrived in the form of a transmission that was ready to be junked. When I was able to find the problem, it woke everyone up, and they realized I *did* have some knowledge, and from that day on, I was accepted as one of the boys.

"There's a fascination with being able to drive a car and know what it's doing, and then seeing the problems repaired. It's a real thrill putting the transmission back in the car, and then driving that same car! If you've ever been involved in this type of work, it's instant gratification. You take the car down the road, and boom, boom, it shifts perfectly, and it's just a thrill!"

Lucille has sought automotive thrills since she was a teenager—she learned to drive her father's truck when she was fourteen years old. "Even at that time, I enjoyed speed and anything to do with driving!" Speed is Lucille's demon. "I've never done any legal racing, never been on a racetrack, but I've had more than a few street races.

"The first new car I purchased was probably my most favorite car of all; a 1966 GTO, burgundy with a black interior; a real muscle car. I bought it when I first became totally immersed in the automotive business. I ordered a special model, and as soon as I picked it up from the dealer, I brought it out to the automotive shop where I was employed, and we power-timed it, so it picked up even more horsepower.

"By that time, I wanted a real high-performance car, because I'd learned to appreciate performance over looks. The GTO was something really new then.

"This car was really great fun driving around in traffic, because you don't normally see an adult woman driving a GTO! I would just sit at a red light, looking nonchalant, and the driver in the car beside me would look at me, and wham, I'd leave them in the dust!

"Everything on that GTO was just exactly what I wanted. I kept it until my first son turned sixteen and was learning to drive. He'd spent his life speeding, with his mother at the wheel! I was really afraid to let him learn on the GTO; there was just too much power for a sixteen year old."

When Lucille set up her own business, she wanted the name of her transmission shop to attract attention, just like her GTO. "I wanted to take advantage of my recognition as a specialist, and to position myself as high-quality, high-tech, a top-notch shop. 'Transmissions by Lucille' sounds like a designer dress! It has turned out to be a very good name for me, and has drawn a lot of attention."

With the GTO long gone, Lucille remains attentive to a car's performance. Today she drives a 1987 Buick Park Avenue. "It suits me. By this time I want a car that has a good ride, and a little bit of luxury. It looks like a really stable, conservative car, with its comfy seats, but of course I chose the package with heavy-duty suspension, bigger wheels, and a little better rear end ratio, so it'll really take off. I have the best of both worlds; a car that really responds, and still gives a good ride.

"When you purchase a car, it has to be a love affair; if you're going to invest in it, its responsiveness is very important. You've got to like how it feels to drive. I would try a few different cars before making a decision. If you are like me, a person who really wants a car to perform, and you buy a car with a low-powered engine, it's very frustrating. It's not enjoyable to drive a car like that.

"I think it's important, when you're in a car as much as most people are, that you feel like you're one with the car. It's not just one thing, like the tires, or the color of the car that's important. You've got to feel that response, whether you're steering or giving it the gas. Then you feel like you and the car are almost one piece, that's what's important. Believe me, when you drive your car, it's an absolute relationship. It's one of the most important relationships in your life."

Lucille Treganowan from Pennsylvania with her Buick Park Avenue in her shop, "Transmissions by Lucille."

In making this car with female images, I wanted to take some of the power back…

What is "very huggable, inviting, non-threatening, and curvaceous with no hard edges?" This is Shelley Buschur's description of her 1971 Karmann Ghia, otherwise known as "Planet Karmann." Shelley is not only a car artist, but a talented metalsmith and nurse-midwife. Planet Karmann is dedicated to Teresa, a twenty-two year old, HIV-positive woman for whom Shelley cared as part of her work in a National Institutes of Health study on women. "It was inspiring, the way Teresa lived her life, knowing she was going to die soon. She made me laugh, even though I only knew her a short time. Midwives, you know, usually take care of low-risk, healthy women. Teresa really changed my life, so I wanted to acknowledge her in some way. I became a midwife because I wanted to empower women by giving them as much control over their health care as possible. Women are amazingly strong and powerful, and somewhere along the way, we're taught to negate that aspect of our lives."

Shelley's ideas on feminine experience influence her life and her art. "My favorite metalwork is a series of brooches that encapsulate women's lives; their titles are badges for unpopular causes. There's a

badge for 'The Bearer of Bad News' which is about breaking up with my boyfriend. My first badge I called 'Menstruation Liberation,' looking at it as a life-giving process. There's a badge titled 'Being Inactive' about barrenness and how fertile you can be if you don't have children, and there's a badge called 'Recalcitrant' for someone who insists upon living in the 1960s, which people accuse me of doing!

"Painting my car was truly empowering. Taking over its whole appearance was a way of making it more my own, and a learning experience. To get these images I posed for photographs, completed drawings from the photos, and then began drawing on the car and tried to work with the curves of the car and the curves of the body. There are suns, stars, planets, meteors, all kinds of celestial things, and there are green women. The idea behind having women of different colors comes from a conversation my car and I were having as we drove down the road. If 'Karmann' had a choice, people and cars could be whatever color they wanted, and women would be comfortable with their bodies, and be good to each other.

"Make your car your own; don't be afraid, and don't let anyone else tell you what you should do. Cars make great canvases."

Shelley Buschur from Texas with her 1971 Karmann Ghia, "Planet Karmann."

I've become a good Samaritan.

I've helped a lot of guys who've broken down on the side of the road…

Artist Alex Coward admits she's a collector. Under the carport of Alex's home sit four cars; one is a daily driver, the others are projects or parts donors. "I've always liked old things. Old houses and old cars are strong. I like the way metal looks; it has character and personality."

Alex's first car was a Plymouth Fury. Little did she realize the consequences of her next automotive purchase. What Alex wanted was a car, and what she got was a relationship. Alex bought her 1972 BMW from a rancher who "told me the engine was not only steam-cleaned, but rebuilt. I thought I could trust him, but when I went to pick up the car, he already had my check, the hood was off, the engine was off to the side; everything was in pieces. I was livid; I knew *nothing* about cars." Once the car was towed on a flatbed trailer, greater infusions of cash were required. Besides the $3,000 Alex spent on the purchase, $1,100 more were needed to put it back together. Nine days later, on the freeway, smoke enveloped her and Alex discovered that the engine's head was cracked.

Alex's education was just beginning. Instead of bringing her car where she requested, the tow truck drivers brought it somewhere else. "My Texas mentality came out; I was so mad. I didn't own a gun, and never have, but I had visions of shooting at the mechanics' feet and making them dance. The car was on the lot for six months. It was always 'ready,' but as soon as I'd arrive, it wasn't. I threw fits, and they didn't have any excuses. Six months later I got my car, and, driving down the freeway, I see my air cleaner bouncing down the street. Things were flying off my car!"

So Alex made one of those life-changing decisions. "I decided then and there to learn about my car, and work on it myself. I asked a lot of questions at a foreign auto shop, and got to be good friends with the counter guy. One day he told me, 'If you're willing to do the actual work, I'll tell you what needs to be done and I'll point out the parts.' Five days a week, after art school, I'd go to the auto shop and learn about my car."

Alex reels off a list of what she's accomplished. "I've put in a transmission cooling system, adjusted my own valves and gaskets, and pulled out my radiator. I've rebuilt my alternator, worked on horns and mufflers, and put in my ignitions. Whatever goes wrong, you ask questions, and you figure it out, you do it, and it's not that hard. The manuals pretty much lay it on the line. Now I do my own tune-ups. You just learn what gauge to use, how to torque it, and you learn the feel of things. It feels really good to work on your car!"

Alex found an unexpected benefit of her mechanical prowess. "I've become a good Samaritan; I've helped a lot of guys who have broken down on the side of the road. I get a lot of pleasure from walking up, asking them what's the matter, and troubleshooting. Usually it's really simple, and it saves them a tow job."

After her beloved BMW, which she had named "Dino" got smashed, Alex bought another, which she named "Dina" to use for parts, and turned Dino into an art car, which she now calls "Thorny Rock and Roll."

"I love terrariums, fish, dinosaurs, and snakes, and a lot of my paintings are raw and reptilian. People always say whatever I do is animal-like. I don't know why, but I wanted these protruding cones sticking out."

Experimentation was part of the process. "I bought champagne flutes and Dixie cups. There are shot glasses up on the nose of the car like warts, and Styrofoam cups, and weird little tequila glasses. There is also a dorsal fin, covered in fiberglass." Color schemes change constantly. "The colors are whatever I get free from Joe's paint and body shop. Thorny Rock and Roll is now taking a turn towards blue, and it's a happier car. I also touch it up with silver and gold spray paint, and I've gotten it down to a science where I can restore a broken cone pretty easily. If you're going to put the effort into making an art car, make it something strong and sturdy, something you can drive through rain, snow, or whatever happens."

Alex credits her mother for her skills and attitude. "My mother taught me to be self-sufficient. She was born with a tool belt around her waist, totally into electrical things; she's gadget-oriented and pretty resourceful. I'm a firm believer that there's positive from each bad situation—you learn, you get stronger. That's the deal with my car."

Alex Coward from Texas with her 1972 BMW, "Thorny Rock and Roll."

It's an awesome feeling to bring such joy and happiness…

Nicole Strine-Goldman never knew she was an artist until the day she took the paintbrush out of her mother's hands. But growing up with a serious amateur race car driver for a father meant she knew about cars. Surrounded by Porsches, she learned about performance and maintenance as a child. "The engines of the cars we owned were impeccably clean; you could eat off our engines. Cars get into your blood. My father taught me how to take care of a car long before I ever owned one. I never even threw my bike down as a kid, I even waxed my bike—and I've never owned an automatic, ever."

After more than a decade of driving various used cars, Nicole didn't have any intention of creating a unique car when she started the search for her first brand new car. "I test-drove sixteen different models at the Honda dealer to make sure that my first new car was going to be exactly what I wanted. I wanted to test everything." What Nicole couldn't imagine or test was driving a car covered with paintings of peacocks and cats, because she drove out of the showroom the owner of "a beautiful, shiny, inconspicuous, sleek, little gray Honda.

"One day, a car artist friend asked, 'When are you going to paint this?' I answered, 'Are you nuts? This is a new car; I wax this car, this car is beautiful, it's in impeccable condition, this is my babe.' I drove it plain, shiny, and gray for a long time."

Eventually, a road trip with friends to St. Louis towing an art car known as "Ripper the Friendly Shark" opened her eyes to the possibilities of automotive art. When they reached St. Louis, Nicole took the passenger seat in a friend's painted Toyota, a car that's driven every day.

A car like "Ripper the Friendly Shark" is fantastic and sculptural, but it is also high maintenance. Riding in a painted art car suited Nicole's style. "I thought, 'I could do this, it's low maintenance, I wouldn't have to worry about people taking things off.' We were driving around and people would beep and wave, and I thought to myself 'What a gas!'

"It's an awesome feeling to bring such joy and happiness. If the car is happy enough, you can't help but laugh and smile. I realized I would *love* a painted car, something bright and original.

"I had never had any formal training in art, so I asked for help from my mother, a trained artist who hadn't painted in seventeen years. We wet-sanded the car for five hours. You don't want to take the paint off, but you take the clear coat off the car, and that really hurt; it hurt so badly! My shiny, beautiful waxed car; the clear coat had kept it so good for so long.

"I *thought* Mom was going to do everything; both of the cats, and the peacock on the hood. She painted the Cheshire cat in two hours. I gave her a glass of wine, she sipped, her little nose turned red, she painted, and we had a blast. We went through mother-daughter bonding like nobody's business!

"We used a sign painters' enamel, not water soluble, but easy to work with. We were lucky with temperature, and got nice thick coats of paint. Every little inch of that car is brush painted! There's not any spray painting! It took us a month in our spare time. If I wasn't sleeping, eating, or bathing, I was painting, and so was Mom.

"Mom painted the Cheshire cat, and I said, 'I wish I could help you.' She asked, 'Why don't you do this one?' I told her, 'Mom I'm not the artist in the family.' She said I didn't give myself enough credit, and asked me to try. Watercolors are a one-shot deal, but the great thing about enamels or oils is, you can paint over them. She started drawing the designs out, while I stood behind her, thinking, 'That doesn't look right; why are you doing it like that?' Finally I said, 'No—wait, give it to me!' So she put the brush in my hand, and I started painting. Two hours later she looked up at me and smiled. Then I knew she had tricked me; she'd done it wrong on purpose!

"The first day it was finished, we took it out in the blaring sunshine, and waited for the reaction. People waved, or honked, gave me a thumbs up. Kids really love it; it's a children's car, and in any parade I will wave at them, rather than their parents, or any good looking men I may see on the side of the road.

"A woman will always do what's necessary to get through life, and some of the best art cars come from women; we are meticulous and methodical, and I do believe in our practical ways. The title of my car, 'Cat's Meow' isn't just about cats; it means 'it's the best—perfection.'

"I painted my car the year before it was paid off, can you imagine a repossession? Having an art car becomes an addiction. I'm addicted to this art car thing—it's a fever! I have to make sure that I always have a job that will give me money to buy the cars I want to create. It will always be part of my life."

Nicole Strine-Goldman from Texas with her 1990 Honda, "The Cat's Meow."

The true test of a car comes after it's five years old...

Viola player Margaret Strange admits, "I like cars that are perfectly square." One day, accompanying a roommate on her automotive search, Margaret stated her preferences to the owner of Western Auto. He led her straight to a beige and gold 1963 Rambler American, saying, "I've got just the car for you."

There was only one problem. Margaret lacked cash. Car ownership, however, would help her to increase her livelihood. A graduate of the New England Conservatory of Music, Margaret plays viola as part of a classical music ensemble at various functions, including weddings. Having a car would allow her to accept gigs farther afield. Margaret struck a deal with the owner. "I worked selling cars, and eventually got my car at cost."

The square car was finally Margaret's. "I didn't really care if I got my driver's license when I turned sixteen. I really couldn't tell one car from another. But now I'm trying to learn as much as I can about the Rambler. I really love the car because it's so different. Sometimes it's even annoying; you just want to drive down the road, and people are yelling out, 'Hey, Hey.'"

Working at a used-car lot has been quite an education. "I get a lot of car advice; why not to lease, how to get a good car cheaply, and the reasons not to finance, unless, of course, you've got money to blow! It's really funny how cheaply you can buy cars. I was able to buy a 1984 Subaru four-wheel-drive model for only $100 for my mother. I had its exhaust fixed for $50, and then drove it to the Hershey, Pennsylvania classic car show, and gave it to my mother for her birthday. She's owned it for over a year and it's still going strong." Margaret is emphatic on the value of a good used car. "American people really think they *need* new cars; it's drilled into you from television everyday, but there is not a twenty-thousand-dollar difference between a new car and a used car. The true test of a car comes after it's five years old."

Since Western Auto is a self-service lot, Margaret spends her spare moments practicing her viola. "Most people who come here know what they're doing. They look at the car, drive it, and then bargain with you on the price. Before I began working here I never knew that there was bargaining room!

"My Rambler was apparently the old lady's kind of car. When I bought it, there were only 72,000 miles on it, not 172,000! It's beige with a gold stripe. It's the economy model, but it has seat belts, which weren't always available, and it has bucket seats that fold down into a kind of bed. It has a two-tone console, so it's the souped-up version of the Rambler you normally see. Once, when I was late for a gig, it did seventy miles per hour, and it was very quiet; you don't even hear its engine. Nothing's gone wrong in a while, and there's always *Hemmings Motor News* for hard-to-find parts.

"When I told my parents about my purchase, they said 'Uh-oh, we had Ramblers when we were growing up, and they *always* fell apart.' But I've been told I could take my Rambler anywhere. I don't want to drive it really long distances because I don't want to waste the miles. I want to have it for as long as I can. Now I know how to jump start a car, change tires, and check fluids, and I can recognize some of the sounds when things go wrong.

"The owner of the car lot says I should sell the Rambler if someone offers me $3,000 for it, but I wouldn't. If I couldn't have this car, I'd probably want a BMW 2002; they're square, and their wheel base design is supposed to be perfect. But I couldn't sell the Rambler, unless someone offered me some ridiculous amount of money, like $10,000, and maybe then I couldn't say no. I'd buy a new bow for my viola, and then buy a car."

Margaret has customized her "Rambling Rose." "I painted 'R's on the wheel rims, so they look shiny and new, and a small red 'V' on the hood ornament, since I'm called 'Viola' here on the lot.

"I can fit five people and two cellos in my Rambler. I like it because it's roomy inside. It looks like a cartoon car, and I like it because it's square."

Margaret Strange from Massachusetts with her 1963 Rambler American, "Rambling Rose."

On the service side, I'm learning more...

Like many women, Jana Mihopoulos waited until her son and daughter entered school before she began looking for a full-time job. She had waitressed, worked in a pharmacy, and even calibrated airplane engines when she married eleven years ago, but these were all part-time jobs. One day, Jana was intrigued by a Saturn commercial. "It was the commercial where the woman bought a Saturn, then decided to sell Saturns so she could show men the vanity mirror. At my interview, when they asked why I wanted to sell cars, I told them it was so I could show guys the vanity mirror!"

Growing up with three older brothers, Jana hung around her father, a diesel mechanic, as he worked on jeeps during his days in the National Guard. "He always gave me those good jobs, like washing the oil pan, and changing tires. But I had absolutely no background for selling cars. I didn't know anything about Saturns, believe me! As a salesperson, I was in the 'bullpen' with seventeen men, but they were great! I sold cars for about a year and a half before the service manager approached me, and asked if I'd like to come into the service side of the dealership as a service consultant.

"I was hesitant at first, but now I really like it. On the service side, it's more consistent, and besides, I'm learning more. All the technicians are a great help, they teach me, and never make me feel out of place. It's harder than sales, much harder. Being 'cross-trained' means I know where the salespeople demand a lot of the service people, especially when they have a delivery. You've got to take care of the customer who's in front of you, so it can be hard to balance."

Jana's service consultant job involves translating for the mechanics from the customers' descriptions of symptoms or noises. "I don't diagnose your problems, but I have to get enough information for the technician to diagnose your problem. I can't just say to the mechanic, 'Oh, there's a noise under the hood.' I try to see where the noise is, and help them with a lot of information. It saves them time, and saves the customer time in diagnostics.

"The mechanics have to write down everything they've done, and I look at it, confirm they've done it, and explain it to the customer. Today people want good service, and want to go somewhere where there are knowledgeable people. They're not going to have me suggest they get their tires rotated if I can't tell them why it's necessary."

Jana is emphatic on the value of reading the hardcover book that is the Saturn owner's manual. "I have so many people come in here who don't know how to set their clocks, or clean their tape players. I show them how, and show them the page in the owner's manual where the instructions are located. I also have people who come in saying, 'My brakes are making a clinking sound.' Right away I know they have anti-lock brake systems because the ABS brakes make a clinking noise at 5 miles per hour while they set themselves. A lot of people don't know that and think something is wrong."

Sometimes maintenance, light bulbs, and wiper blades are all that's required. "When you sell people a car, they're very happy, but when they come into the service department, you're going to have to take more money out of their pocket. They know they have to have their oil changed, but they don't *want* to pay for it! People come in with blown light bulbs, and whether they're male or female, I'll change the bulb. I had a man look at me as if to say, 'Oh, is that all you do?' He was embarrassed, and I kind of loved it! The same thing happens when I replace the wiper blades. Occasionally I have people who don't want to deal with me because I'm a woman. They say they *have* to see the service manager. If I need to, I'll get him, but usually we resolve whatever it is. I answer their questions, and I guess I do pretty well. They come back to thank me!"

Meanwhile, Jana learned so much about serpentine belts, timing chain guides, and polymer panels that when it came time for her to purchase a new car, she picked a blue-green Saturn SL2. Jana was a minivan driver, with a sports car fantasy. "I had been the homemaker, driving the minivan. I had to talk my husband into the car, and show him why I thought the Saturn would be good for us. I told him all about the engine, and now he loves the engine's performance. He drives the minivan now, but he'll take my Saturn if he can get his hands on it. Even though we both pay for it, it's really *my* car. I get in there, and I want the seat to be in the position I left it, and like my radio stations set. I would have loved a sports coupe, but I went with the sedan. I enjoy shifting the manual transmission, so I feel sporty, and it handles just like a sports car."

Jana thinks nothing of getting in the car to drive several hundred miles on her own, and offers her own list of advice for women. "You have to have confidence in what you're driving. I feel very confident in my car; with the shift I can handle anything, and I have a lot of control."

Jana has earned the highest customer service rating of the technicians at the Saturn dealership where she works. "From sales to service, I want to treat people the way I want to be treated. I had never worked full-time, and my job was hard on my family at first, but they've adjusted. I work a lot of hours, but I've never loved a job before. I've been here the longest of any other woman in sales or service, and I love it. I told them I'll be here forever. I'm here to stay."

Jana Mihopoulos from Rhode Island at her job in the service department of a Saturn dealership.

When I first started working on the car someone said
I must be having one hell of a menopause…

Thousands of tiny Barbie Doll shoes, thin sheets of gold leaf, and pieces of mirrored glass, combined with Armor Keller's artistry, transformed her 1980 Toyota station wagon into "The Magic City Golden Transit," an ongoing art car project she started in 1989. Says Armor, "It expresses my interest in changes and aging. My station wagon still ran well, but it needed a change, much like a woman 'needs' a face lift. I decided not to have a face lift, but to give the car one instead. As it changed and became rejuvenated, so did I.

"When I first started working on the car, which was a natural extension of my painting, someone said I must be having one hell of a menopause! I think growing older gives you permission to do something perhaps you had always wanted to do but did not, because it was not proper for a 'Southern Lady.' Now I put on my special driving outfit and cruise around town in my Cinderella golden coach, not worrying about changes in life, but enjoying and expressing my creativity."

Armor plugs in the strands of tiny Christmas lights decorating the car's interior, and points out the

red, white, and blue flowers recently added for the car's participation in Birmingham's welcome parade for Miss America. Besides the gold leaf surfaces covered with mirrored glass are beads contributed by a Birmingham glassblower. The thousands of plastic Barbie doll shoes were discovered at a yard sale, and the leatherette suitcases Armor received for her eleventh birthday are covered in gold, trimmed with beads, and are strapped onto the top of the car.

"The car works its magic by bringing a smile to the faces of all who see it, and by bringing art to people who never go to museums or galleries, showing them how art and the everyday world connect. It's an extension of my artwork. I probably would not have done it had I not been an artist. I keep thinking of it as kind of a mobile sculpture. It's very tactile, though all the broken glass makes it kind of dangerous to touch. It's fun to leave the car where I can watch it and see people react.

"The car needs constant attention. I'm always replacing something or gluing something onto it. It's definitely high maintenance. I've spent a fortune just on glue. Most people are afraid to do something different or take a chance. Driving this car is like getting to play dress-up every day."

Armor is delighted with the liberating effect of her car on her own life. "I get out of my role as a wife and mother, and become the artist I really am. For one thing, you can't really be in a bad mood and drive the art car. You've got to be willing to go along with the excitement it creates and accept the attention."

Armor Keller from Alabama with her 1980 Toyota station wagon, "The Magic City Golden Transit."

Motorcycling is my freedom…

Jodi Solomon confesses, "I've become a big gearhead; I can talk motorcycles for hours, and I subscribe to about eight different motorcycle magazines." But it's only recently that Jodi confessed her secret passion to her family. "Everybody's very protective, because of motorcycling's bad reputation. My brother also has a motorcycle, but it's kept a secret in the family. It wasn't until after my mother passed away last year that I finally told my father. He was very good about it."

High school offered Jodi her first chance to climb on the back of a friend's motorcycle. "I loved it, loved it, loved it, but my parents said 'No, no, no, stay off that bike!'" She obeyed their wishes for a brief period, before purchasing a Honda 350 motorcycle of her own.

Eventually Jodi moved to Boston, outgrew her first bike, and cultivated friendships with motorcycle-owning males. "We used to do a lot of traveling together, but I was tired of riding on the backs of *their* bikes." Enrollment in the Motorcycle Safety Foundation's weekend course affirmed Jodi's desire for greater motorcycling power. Jodi owned a Honda 650 for only six months, then she succumbed to the lure of a BMW 650.

Jodi cautions women to be respectful of motorcycles' power. "When I first began taking day trips by myself I used to be so scared that I wouldn't sleep the night before. Once I got on my bike, the nervousness would evaporate. I think men's attitudes towards riding may be a bit more cavalier. Whenever I plan a ride, I always watch the weather report. Men wouldn't think about the weather; they'd just get on and go. On a motorcycle, it's important to be focused and concentrate. You're always wondering what's going to happen next; wet leaves, gravel, oil in the road, or any of a million things. I don't ever just randomly hop on my bike, so it's a different way of living.

"Every time I come back from a long trip, I always say, 'Thank you,' to my motorcycle for bringing me back safely. On the highway, you're often going faster than it seems. Once in a while I'll crank it up, but I concentrate more on the style of my riding, and how I will go into my next turn, than on how fast the scenery can whiz by. I like to take my time and absorb everything."

Jodi absorbed breathtaking autumn scenery from the seat of her bike as she traveled through ravines and canyons on a journey from Las Vegas to the Grand Canyon. "Doing eight or nine hours a day would be exhausting to some, but to me, it's exhilarating and challenging. You hug the road, and your body becomes one with the motorcycle. It's titillating and thrilling at the same time. At the end of the day, you've used not only your physical capabilities, but your mental capabilities.

"There's a mind-body-spirit connection with the motorcycle, which I don't get from any of the other sports I've done. I run a company with ten employees. It can be extraordinarily stressful, so my motorcycle is the way I find freedom. I find peace riding the country roads. As a woman who lives in the city, who seeks the solace of the woods and Mother Earth, motorcycles have enabled me to be by myself in wooded areas and feel safe.

"I work really hard, and I want to play as hard as I work. I'm willing to take the risks, and go out to the edge, but I'm really conscious of safety." Jodi offers a few safety tips for women curious about the motorcycling world. "Enroll in the Motorcycle Safety Foundation course; it helps you know what to expect; do some test riding, and remember you grow into your motorcycles very quickly.

"It's really important what you do with your life, and what helps you make the most of it. Motorcycling has enhanced my life; it's made me take more risks, as a person, in business, and in my practice of martial arts.

"On the back of my helmet is a "NO FEAR" sticker, and it's true. I can't go through life being scared about all the things that may or may not occur. I've really got to savor and be grateful for all the moments I have on this earth. Motorcycling is my freedom."

Jodi Solomon from Massachusetts with her BMW 650 motorcycle.

It's something other than a factory item, it's personalized…

Suzahne Riendeau drove 16,000 miles during a thirteen-week road trip from New England to the Southwest. For ten years, Suzahne traveled the globe, visiting Africa, Greece, Turkey, and most of Europe, but she'd never driven Route 66, or toured the Grand Canyon.

Three years ago, she decided it was time to buy a used car, and hit the road to see all she'd missed. "My romantic notion of a cross-country trip included a car with character, maybe a classic or a convertible." But a 1989 Toyota Tercel with only 84,000 miles turned up for sale. Suzahne hesitated. "I thought it was boring. I would love to buy an old car. But I also knew I needed a car that was not going to leave me stranded with 100 miles of desert in every direction. This car was in great condition; it had the luxury of air conditioning, and it was a bargain, so I *knew* it was stupid not to grab it. Even today, with 139,000 miles on it, I've never had any problems.

"People are usually impressed with women traveling alone, they think it's very brave, but I really like traveling alone. Usually I buy little mementos from the places I visit, so on this trip I bought bumper stickers. The first sticker came from New Orleans, a city I love. But I kept thinking I would just use my car for my road trip and sell it when I returned. Then, one day, I thought to myself, 'Of course I'm not going to sell it; it's a great car!' As soon as I made the decision not to resell the Toyota I plastered the first sticker on the bumper."

For the first three weeks of her trip, Suzahne visited friends and family. Her last family visit was with her aunt in Bryant, Texas. "As soon as I left her place, I was really in travel mode, camping, and visiting the national monuments, seeing the Carlsbad Caverns, going to Flagstaff, buying little mementos, keeping a journal and collecting stamps from each place. Yellowstone was fabulous! I'd accumulated maybe ten bumper stickers; they already covered the bumper, and still I had more stickers, so one day I just slapped that Painted Desert bumper sticker on the side of the car and that was it! I thought, 'OK, I'm going to make this car more interesting to look at than a hundred thousand other Toyota Tercels." Super glue transformed the interior, beginning with a tiny lobster to represent New England, and culminating in an assortment of buttons and "stuff."

"My car was a little place I lived inside of for most of thirteen weeks, driving for hours and hours at a time, so I wanted to make it into something. When I was camping by myself, my car would be parked with a lot of different family cars, and the little kids flocked to it. As soon as the kids came over, their parents would follow, tell me where they were from or where they'd been, and sometimes ask if I wanted to come over for some supper! My vehicle is an expression of my mentality, and people want to talk to me."

It's not only supper and discussions her car inspires. "People leave notes under my windshield wipers, they leave stickers, and sometimes they even put stickers on, which I think is pretty rude." Suzahne offers a few words of bumper sticker etiquette, "Do *not* put the sticker of *your* favorite band on someone else's car. You may love the band, but I may not." Suzahne wanted her car to entertain, not offend. "I didn't want it to be 'in your face' political, but it does offend some people.

"Three different people have come up to me, and said, quite seriously, 'You know you've ruined the resale value of your car!' I mean, that just says it all, right there! It's a good litmus test of people. I find a lot of older people really like my car. I've had so many little old ladies standing outside my car at the supermarket, amazed that anyone would do such a thing, but they like it; they laugh and wave, beep, or stop at a red light and comment. If you had a 'normal' car, you'd never have people reaching out. People have to say *something*. As far as I'm concerned that's great, because I'm having some kind of interaction and stimulating people.

"I'm really glad I extended my traveling days beyond my college years. As I began getting older I began thinking about what kind of lifestyle I could have. Once you're no longer college-aged, people ask, 'What are you living like that for?' As you get older, it's no longer a stage you're going through; it's a statement about who you are. I wanted a lot of different experiences and contact with a lot of different people."

Suzahne's travels came to a sudden halt when her father had an accident from which he is now recovering. "During that year, I knew I had to settle; I had to stop traveling; and I realized I'd been traveling for a long time." Once Suzahne stopped traveling, the bumper stickers on the Toyota never let her forget her relationship with the road or her car.

Suzahne, now the owner of a housecleaning business, admits attachment not only to her car. "Personally, I have this kind of relationship with almost everything I own. I don't want to own just a bunch of items; I don't care about owning things; I care about their significance to me. My house is like my car; full of goofy, little, sentimental things, gifts, or items I stuck in my pocket while traveling, and when I pull them out, there's a little story I remember.

"People sometimes think it's silly to love your car, but why not? The same people will say, 'Oh, I love that chair, my grandmother used to have that chair in her house,' well, that's the same thing. To be surrounded by items of significance that are more than utilitarian enriches your life. If you have creative urges, but you don't have the time or ability to put 100 percent into them, you can still be creative through your dress, or you can decorate your house or your car; you can do anything.

"If you put enough energy into it, people respond. They may not be comfortable with it, but it's something other than a factory item; it's personalized. Everybody wants to see evidence of the human beings around them. It's goofy; I didn't know what I was intending to do until after it started. It's just me coming out in another way, so I'm looking forward to the next 80,000 miles."

Suzahne Riendeau from Massachusetts with her 1989 Toyota Tercel.

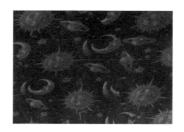

I was the first female in the Houston school district allowed in the shop classes...

Darlene Kirk credits a reluctant high school principal for the skills she used to rescue her 1976 Buick Apollo Skylark, which had a mere 20,000 miles on its six-cylinder engine. "When I was in high school in 1971, I wanted to take shop and drafting, but they never had any girls in the classes. When I requested those classes, both my parents had to come down to school and talk with the principal. I told him I wanted to open a craft shop someday, and he decided to let me in. So in 1971, I was the first female the Houston school district allowed in the shop classes. Drafting was great. The day after I began, word got out, so they had to let the other girls in. I was glad that I opened the door for other females. The classes gave me a well-rounded basis for arts and crafts, even though I never opened a craft shop!"

Darlene confesses she wasn't looking for another craft project, "just mechanically sound transportation. "Originally, the Skylark was owned by an elderly friend of my mother-in-law's. He couldn't see very well; consequently, he kept bumping into everything. When I bought it for $500 no one could see any potential in the car, but little by little I got it into shape. As Jerry Seinfeld says, 'The

car with the different color doors has the right of way!' People would be killing themselves to get out of my way. They didn't know I drive like a granny."

Once its body was restored and its exterior healed with indigo blue paint, Darlene turned her eye towards its interior. "I've always done craft projects, but it was a big deal to take on a car." But necessity and marital harmony forced the issue. "The car's headliner was falling down; and when my six-foot-three husband drove the car, it would sit on the top of his head. 'This is never going to work,' I thought, and the headliner was horrible blue vinyl with tiny pinpoint holes. We tried stapling, but it didn't last. It was just a big mess, then one day I got REALLY mad, and went out there and ripped it all out, so then I HAD to do something. The car had this corrugated cardboard top that was an unpainted canvas, waiting for something to happen."

Darlene spotted the solution to her headliner problems at a local gift shop amongst the party decorations and invitations. She bought five rolls of celestial gift wrapping and her vision was complete.

Only one obstacle remained. "Houston's weather is 90 percent humidity most of the time, so I waited until there were perfectly clear skies on a dry day, and I'd take off work and run home and decoupage a little bit at a time." Darlene's celestial headliner took "four full days of perfect, perfect weather to complete. I was lying down on the seats, with all this glue, looking up at the ceiling as if I were Michelangelo. Once I got the headliner done, one thing led to another, and I ended up stenciling and painting the floor mats, and the door handles. It's real freeform, but I'm kind of compulsive, and I like symmetry, so it was hard for me to do some of the comets and shooting stars. If you see my car driving down the street, you have no idea. You just think it's a classic 1970s American car, until you sit inside."

Darlene Kirk from Texas inside her 1976 Buick Apollo Skylark.

I thought I would make it as theft-proof as possible…

Alison Darrow explains, "When I first bought this car, it was nearly new, a polite, little, 1983 Toyota, mostly gold with black trim. It was the archetypal little old lady car." Alison took her cue from a friend who always named her cars after virtues; a Puritan tradition. "Her name is Tenacity, because being tenacious usually works eventually!"

Vermont native Alison moved to the big city, and found a beautiful artist's studio with great light, but she knew, "car theft was a possibility, and Toyotas were one of the cars of choice for thieves. I thought I would make it as theft-proof as possible without laying out a lot of money for an alarm system." When her car was broken into, her first solution was "the baby doll defense."

"I had about twenty-five baby dolls from the Salvation Army thrift store. These dolls were NOT cute; they'd been loved to death, their hair was sticking out, and they were covered in crayon. They were really kind of gruesome, so I left them in the car's back seat, trying to make the car look as if a psycho owned it. When people kept breaking into my car, instead of replacing the glass, I began stuffing the baby dolls into the window. For a while it was a really scary looking car."

Still, "Tenacity" was getting broken into every week. "It felt like such a violation. A car is a private space; it's your little rolling kingdom. The Toyota is not a glamorous car, but it would be great to 'part out,' and would be heading right to a chop shop, so I figured painting it up like this was the best I could do!"

Alison had already practiced her stenciling skills designing T-shirts and other items. "My father's one of those guys who, when you ask him what he wants for Christmas, says, 'Socks and underwear.' So I bought him boxer shorts and stenciled them with a trout design. He loved them, and wore them to death." Naturally, when it came to painting her car, her thoughts turned to stenciling.

"Maple leaves seemed easiest, so I picked up some leaves, made stencils from them, and used as many colors of gold spray paint as I could find. They're blowing in the wind, and I pointed them towards the back of the car, so they'd look as if they're in motion. I'd always wanted to paint a car, but never had the nerve!"

It wasn't only nerve Alison needed, but time. "It takes an incredibly long time to paint a car; I worked in my parents' partly heated Vermont garage over Thanksgiving. It takes much longer than you'd think. It took me three full days to do the first paint job. When my parents saw it, I think they were a bit nonplused. My brother-in-law loves it; he saw it and burst out laughing, and a number of friends said, 'You finally did it, I'm so proud of you!' Before its paint job, it really was a scary car, but now I guess I've toned it down. I'm going for 'beauty' more than 'psycho.'"

But apparently, in some people's minds, Tenacity Toyota was still psycho. "A lot of people really seem to disapprove of painting a car. People stare at me all the time, and I always get the right of way at intersections. People look at it, and think, 'This woman's insane! If she could do *that* to her car, just think what she'll do to mine if I get in her way!'" In Alison's former job as a project manager for an environmental services laboratory, Tenacity caused a bit of trouble. "I wasn't allowed to park my car out front if there was an important client coming; I had to park it where it wouldn't be too obtrusive! It's a serious field, and everything has to be correct." And on a road trip to Canada with her boyfriend, "as soon as Customs took one look at my car, they pulled us over, went through our luggage, even searched inside the door panels, although why they thought a courier would drive such a blatant, gaudy car, I don't know!" Alison sighs, "You can't be anonymous in an art car."

Alison admits she loves her car. "There's something very American about having a love affair with your car. I get a car, get to know it, settle in, and I have no desire to get rid of it. One thing you decide when you begin to paint your car is that you will have the car until it dies."

Alison Darrow from Massachusetts with her 1983 Toyota, "Tenacity."

I realized that I owned one thing, and it was the car…

One of Washington, D.C.'s tourist attractions can't be found in a guidebook, and it has nothing to do with any elected official. If you're lucky, you might catch a glimpse of it on the street. As writer Amy Dickinson rides through the streets of Washington, D.C., horns honk appreciatively, windows roll down, and people yell out, "What *is* it?"

"It" is a 1967 Morris Minor 1000, Amy's first and only car. After living in England for eighteen months, Amy says, "I found a dealer who sold restored Morris automobiles. I put my five-week-old baby on the desk while I drove around the block just to make sure I could shift with my left hand. What really sealed the deal was this small green dome Christmas-style light bulb on the arm of the turn signal. I saw that little green light, and I just said 'Wow, it's a done deal!'"

As it turned out, the Morris wasn't destined to remain in London much longer. "My husband and I divorced; it broke my heart, it was a terrible divorce, especially with the baby. I realized that I owned only one thing, and it was the car, so when I decided to return to the United States with Emily, there was never a doubt of bringing it.

"I had the steering wheel, pedals and gear shift moved to the other side (they forgot to move the bright and the dimmer switches; they're still way out of reach on the right). Our apartment was empty. My husband was going to Moscow, and I was going to Washington, D.C. There were two huge moving vans, each pointed in opposite directions. We had split our possessions, and there was still room in my container for the Morris, so they drove it right into the container, with my bureau, my clothes, and my books, and that's how it traveled across the ocean. Several months later, when they drove the car out of the moving van, it started up like a charm. It was my first day in this new apartment, in a new city, and when I saw that car come off the moving van and how it started up right away, I decided that my luck had changed and that my karma was really good, and it's been great!

"The great thing about the Morris is, I can crank it to get it started. For instance, last winter when it was so cold nobody could get their car started, the Morris was fine. It almost always starts instantly, but if it doesn't there's an actual crankshaft I stick through the front of the car. I can crank it just like an old Model T, and I've done that in a cocktail dress and heels. It sits in the garage, looking like a toddler, all plump and ready to go. When it starts, we pat it and yell, 'Good job!' We treat it well; we love it, appreciate it, and respect it. I really believe in that. I'm one of those people who believes that if you treat your things well—with a lot of respect and courtesy—they'll never let you down."

Of course, good karma needs to be supported. "My mechanic warned me that the suspension was going, and I was concerned that I would leave the wheels behind at some point, so I found a British car specialist. The assessment was free. I feared the worst—that it was terminal, the equivalent of a stroke—but I agreed to triage, to do the things that will keep this car safe and on the road. The Morris has seat belts, but they're like tying yourself in with a shoelace; in the back where my daughter sits, I have regulation seat belts. When the windshield wipers work, they squirt little streams of water over the top of the car. Luxury and the Morris are mutually exclusive terms. We drive around in this sweatbox in the summer; we get out, and the sweat has formed a little pool. In winter, the heater blows out a little two-inch stream of heat. It's like a blow dryer that's about to die.

"Maybe I like to stand out. This car has really enhanced me in a way that I don't know what I'd do if I didn't have it. I lead kind of a solitary life; I'm a writer. I spend a lot of time alone, and when I get in the Morris, and I go out onto the streets, I'm somebody, you know."

Amy Dickinson and her daughter, Emily, from Washington, D.C., with her 1967 Morris Minor 1000.

I was really organized so I didn't have any parts left over…

The designer of Funky Frocks clothing, Hannah Kopacz rescued her beloved Barbie-doll pink 1962 Ford Fairlane from her brother five years ago when it was still Corinthian white. "It didn't go fast enough for him, even after he'd rebuilt its transmission."

The Ford was just what Hannah had been looking for, only she didn't know it yet. "I didn't know about mechanical things, but I figured if anything happened, my brother would fix it. Then he moved, and I had to learn how to fix my own car. Now it's so much better, because I can go *anywhere*. I have my own set of tools, painted pink, of course, and a pink toolbox that matches my car's pink engine."

Hannah's family joined forces to help her through a difficult automotive season after the Fairlane's front grille was ruined in an accident. "I fixed the dent on its side, and found a new grille by looking through *Hemmings Motor News*. My brother found me a new exhaust manifold at a junkyard, and my mother bought me a new radiator for my birthday."

Once the Ford Fairlane was healed, Hannah and her boyfriend traveled across the United States on an automotive mission to Richardson Ford, Oklahoma City, where her car had originated.

"The dealership was still standing, but they were completely clueless about my car. They didn't keep paperwork from that long ago, and were amazed when we showed up; they didn't even think their dealership had been around that long!"

Wherever she traveled from there, Hannah's pink Fairlane was the center of attention. "It stole the show! In California, when I drove through the huge Redwood drive-through tree, people stopped what they were doing to take pictures of my car. Everywhere we stopped, people would start singing 'Pink Cadillac,' which gets really irritating after awhile, especially since it's a Ford!"

Hannah grew up without a car in the family. "We lived in the city, near public transportation. I didn't care about cars until I got mine. But I don't name it because that would be like naming a part of myself.

"With an older car, you have to be ever-vigilant. I've replaced the universal joints and the shocks," and a few years ago Hannah installed the engine from a 1965 Mustang into her Ford Fairlane. "You take all the stuff—like the different pumps—off the old engine and put them on the new engine, with the bolts that hold things together; it's easy. I labeled everything, and put it in baggies, and was really organized so I didn't have any parts left over.

"I'm always willing to try anything on my car, even if that means it will be out of commission for a few days. After all, this is my first car, and it will be my last!"

Hannah Kopacz from California with her 1962 Ford Fairlane.

I'm an outsider trying to represent an experience with something that is held sacred by another culture…

Beverly Hayes says, "My father had always said you cannot have a Bug, there's no engine up front, and you'll get squished, so I always wanted one." Years later, grimy and sweaty after a day spent planting trees along a bayou, Beverly's boyfriend, Brian, turned to her and asked, "If you could have any car in the world, what would you want?"

Beverly said, "A Volkswagen Bug. I've always wanted one." Beverly and Brian came home and cleaned up a bit, then took off. "We turned into this neighborhood, and there was a little yellow VW Bug. Knowing I loved it, Brian bought it, and told me it was my birthday present. Driving home was so much fun!"

Beverly's co-workers at the *Houston Chronicle* have a variety of opinions. "Some say, 'God, Beverly, this is a twenty-seven-year-old car!' I'm always putting stuff in; it's a money pit, some of my friends and co-workers think it's really cool, and some of them think I'm crazy.

"Everyone at the paper knew I liked buffalo, so one day about three years ago, when a story came in

about the birth of a female white buffalo in Janesville, Wisconsin, they knew it would grab me. This farmer had a little herd of buffalo, and one morning, he discovered the female had had this white baby. She's not an albino, but a white buffalo; they have dark eyes, but the entire body is white. The town reporter did the story, sent it out on the wire, and it became huge, because the white buffalo is sacred to the Native American nations.

"According to legend, in the beginning the people had no direction or laws. The legend involves two young hunter boys, and the beautiful woman who came to them. She gave them information about the plants, the herbs, and their spirituality. Then she turned into a buffalo, first a black buffalo, then a red buffalo, then a yellow buffalo, and finally, a white buffalo. When the female white buffalo returns she is to unify the nations and bring everybody together. All the colors of the world, the red, the yellow, the black, and the white will come together and there will be peace.

"I *had* to see this buffalo. As we neared Janesville, Brian asked me, 'What do you expect; what do you think is going to happen?' As a joke, I said, 'I'll be disappointed if the buffalo doesn't look straight at me!' Behind the farmer's house were peacocks and burros and in the back of the barn were the buffalo. Hanging all along the gate were offerings people had left to the buffalo; handmade silver jewelry, letters, feathers, and beautiful bead work. Sixty or seventy people were milling about. The white buffalo was lying down with her mother. As I walked up to a gap in the gate, she got up and walked straight to me. She stood there looking at me as if she understood me. Her mother eventually hustled her back, but I was just floating around for a while after the buffalo came to me.

"I started thinking about how best to express what I had seen at Janesville. One day, driving my car, 'Buffalo Bug' came to me. I wanted to incorporate the white buffalo's message for unity and peace, but without trivializing it. I talked with several Native American women about the design, and what not to use, since I didn't want to use anything that was sacred or religious to Native Americans. I'm an outsider trying to represent an experience with something that is held sacred by another culture and I really did not want to offend.

"The women loved the idea. I used the car as a template really; I just took the pieces of material and sort of cut them to the car. Eight yards of painted red, black, yellow, and white denim cover the bug. A galloping herd of one hundred crayon-colored buffalo are thundering over the top. It was a unifying experience because all these different people created the herd during workday breaks, small parties, and quiet evenings. There were people who had done nothing like that in years. Kids, friends, family, co-workers, and eager strangers all colored the buffalo. People were participating in art, even though crayons and white paper are such a simple form. As adults, some people with bad childhood art experiences were still frightened of coloring the buffalo wrong, and then the grumpy curmudgeon newspaper editors would see the crayons and the buffalo, and say, 'Oh cool, let me at it!'

"Eventually there were so many offerings left at the gate in Janesville they could not add any more. A medicine man was called. He took the offerings and burned them, so the ashes would drift up to the sky. The window treatments represent my experience of the gate, and the plants on the wheels represent the Great Plains where huge herds of buffalo once flourished.

"There is something so unusual about this buffalo, now named 'Miracle,' and knowing how much she means to people. Today, you think about all the things people worship. Even people who aren't religious worship something, whether it's sports or television, and these things have no real connection to the nature of life. To think that thousands of people here in the United States can look to this animal for inspiration seems so basic and hopeful.

"The Bug gets lots of reactions. Kids love it; they all want to touch the car. I feel totally free driving, and I remember the feeling I got driving my first car, that this is the best thing ever, to be on my own, and do whatever I want."

Beverly Hayes from Texas with her Volkswagen Beetle, "Buffalo Bug."

Never, ever, did I think I would be driving a truck…

As love affairs go, they're still in the honeymoon stage. This particular relationship is only a few months old, but Rhonda Simpson prepared for it each and every day over the past five years.

The object of Rhonda's affection requires constant upkeep, deep pockets, complex skills, responsible behavior and infusions of $125 every other day. Still, Rhonda is ecstatic about her eighteen-wheel, twenty-seven foot long, shiny, black Mack truck; the truck she will own free and clear in five more years.

Rhonda says, "Never, ever, did I think I would be driving a truck!" But one day, a roommate's ex-boyfriend stopped by for a visit. Big, burly, Otis the truck driver was pretty pleased with himself. "He'd been on the road for five weeks, and there he was, all happy waving five big paychecks in front of my face."

At the time, Rhonda earned her living selling clothing and bric-a brac at flea markets and working as a dishwasher. "I was thinking of going into nursing, but that would take years, and I needed something I could do quickly; like NOW! Washing dishes isn't where I fit! That very weekend, I visited the trucking school. Bing, bang, boom, I showed up Saturday morning, and Monday morning started classes. I just did it!"

Rhonda couldn't know everything she was letting herself in for during the next eight months. "On the first day, I walked into this big garage, and there stood this HUGE truck they used to show you all the parts. Standing next to this thing I was just totally intimidated. I'm thinking, 'This thing is BIG; I don't know.' But after a while, I was into it and I tried to learn everything I could.

"The school was great for me because I didn't know anything mechanically, and I learned all about how the brake chambers and air systems work. You *need* to know these things. If you're on the road, and break down, you need to tell the mechanic what you think is wrong, because he can't bring the whole garage to you.

"There was lot of classroom work and test-taking, but the rest of it was hands-on. It was thrilling! Trying to back the truck up the very first time was insane, but they teach you, you learn, and now it's second nature; it's just like getting up in the morning."

Eight months after she gazed at the giant truck in the garage, Rhonda graduated as one of the top students in her class. As soon as she was awarded her trucker's cap, she was ready to roll. There was only one problem. She had her license, she had the skills, but she had no practical experience. "I got writer's cramp writing resumes. Wherever I went, wherever I saw a truck, I applied. People told me, 'You have no experience, even if you have your license, there's no way we're going to hire you!' I was really disappointed; I didn't think I was going to get a job. If nobody gives me a break, how am I going to get experience?"

Perseverance finally paid off. "I called the union hall, and unbelievably, about two days later they called back, told me to be at S&R Construction at six o'clock the next morning, and from then on, it was unbelievable. The guys were really nice; they helped me learn what I needed. In school, we were practicing hauling box trailers for freight, and now I was working with dump trailers that go up 100 feet in the air. I love construction. I've operated backhoes and I've delivered gravel, asphalt, dirt, loam, sandstone, everything that's needed for construction."

Besides, it's a vital job. "People don't realize that if there weren't any trucks on the road, we wouldn't have homes, we couldn't go to stores, we wouldn't have sewer systems; you can't even imagine all the things trucks haul."

Still, it's never easy being a truck driver. "A lot of people think truck driving is great, all you do is drive, but it's a lot of work. Sometimes you have real heavy loads, and you have to disconnect them, and crank up the landing gear. The different loads also affect how much stopping distance you have. People don't realize a truck can't stop right away. People don't want to be behind a truck, so some will get in front of you at any cost; they'll cut in front of you and then stop, while you're panicking. Hopefully, you're always looking ahead. You have to be totally aware and alert; always, always, always!"

But if you don't have your own truck, it puts you at the bottom of the list for the long-term jobs. "With your own truck, you've really got a shot; the work is more steady." While a trucking student, and even while working for the construction company, Rhonda dreamed about owning her own truck. Less than a year ago, when the company's personnel director heard about a new Department of Transportation (D.O.T.) program to help women and minority group members enter the construction business, he knew he had just the right person in Rhonda.

After a series of rigorous interviews and completion of the requisite paperwork, Rhonda is justifiably proud to be the first participant in the D.O.T. program. They struck a financing deal with Mack Truck so Rhonda would eventually own her truck. An interest-free loan was arranged for a down payment and to help her secure all the required permits. Rhonda had just the right combination of skills and entrepreneurial spirit the D.O.T. was hoping to find.

Over at the Mack dealership, Rhonda pondered the huge purchase. "One truck was red, with a bigger motor, and a few other accessories mine doesn't have, but obviously, that's more money, so I went with this one. It's black, has a smaller engine, and not as much air ride all the way around, but it was a lot cheaper, so I went with what could do the job, and not all the fancy stuff."

Of course, Rhonda's not flashing those big paychecks around yet. For the next five years, she'll be paying off the $120,000 note on her shiny new truck and dump trailer. Rhonda will then own her Solid Slate Trucking free and clear.

Even with five years of trucking experience under her belt, Rhonda found that owning your own truck is a whole different kettle of fish. "At first I had no clue. There are taxes for this, taxes for that; you have to keep track of everything. It was just a little bit overwhelming! I'd go to work, come home, wash the truck, fuel it up, and then have to take care of all the records. But now things are starting to come a little bit easier."

Rhonda doesn't even mind all the maintenance involved. "I grease the truck every week; there are a million different fittings. Naturally, I check the belts, the fluids; the thirty-eight quarts of oil, and I check underneath the truck, too. Just yesterday, I brought my truck in so they could adjust the play on the clutch. I got down there with them and saw what they did, so now I can do it. I keep an eye on the tires; and tighten the lug nuts. I have to do it by hand; an air compressor would be great!"

Two eighty-four gallon gas tanks need constant feeding. "When I was first breaking the truck in, I'd get three to four miles per gallon, which is insane; it hurts. Now I'm getting four to five miles a gallon. That's about $125 every other day. It would be wonderful to get mileage like a car, but that's the business," Rhonda says with a smile.

"There's a lot of power, operating the dump truck, that engine is so big, strong and powerful, and when the dump truck goes up, and lifts that forty-thousand-pound load, it's unbelievable. It's not easy sometimes. You run into a lot of physical things, not that women can't do them, because naturally we can, but it's just a lot on you physically sometimes. Because the money's good in construction, the competition is tough, so you have to be good and strong." When Rhonda pored through the dictionary for possible business names, "Solid Slate Trucking" spoke to her. "It shows people I'm strong, and on an even keel."

Rhonda has earned her solid skills and experience, and she has encouraging words for any woman considering trucking. "When you're first starting out, don't give up. When you've got guys pushing you back, not wanting you to be in trucking, ignore it. If this is what you want, you just have to do it, and not pay attention to what anybody says. Pay attention to your truck, pay attention to everything you need to learn, and know enough about your truck to be safe. I try not to intimidate the guys: I'm not there to race, I'm there to work. They see you on the road, and they have to pass you, and that's okay; I let them go, because I'm going to get there too."

Rhonda Simpson from Rhode Island with her eighteen-wheel, twenty-seven-foot, Mack truck.

I don't care what age you are, if you decide you want to drive, do it…

"If you want to learn to drive, DON'T let your husband teach you!" At age forty-five Belinda Ortiz is learning to drive for the first time. She's the proud owner of a brand new Adirondack Green Saturn named "Marjorie," and barely six weeks away from her driving test. "Go to driving school! You'll learn more, and you WILL eventually get your license. When you're being taught by someone you know, you're a nervous wreck."

After a few stressful sessions with her husband, Louis, Belinda signed up for driving lessons. "The lessons cost $23 per hour—not bad. The instructor gets in, puts you behind the wheel, gives you the fundamentals. He tells you what to do; he talks to you the whole time you're driving. If you make an error he tells you; you don't have to worry about hollering. Then he makes you do that very same thing two or three times until you actually get it."

Even a rainstorm couldn't even keep Belinda away from her driving lesson. "At first it made me very nervous to be driving in so much rain, but the instructor kept making me go, and by the time I finished, he had me going on the back roads and the highway!

"When I was driving with my husband, he might not say anything, but he'd get kind of all scrunched up. I asked, 'What did I do wrong now?' He said, 'Nothing, nothing, nothing,' but I knew I had done something wrong; he just didn't want to say. You get in more arguments and it's just not worth it!

"I'm from Philadelphia, so that's where I'm going to go for my first road trip. The thing is, we'd never had a new car, we'd always had a piece of junk my husband and daughters drove, that got us from point A to point B. About four years ago, I saw a Saturn in a parking lot, and I thought it was gorgeous. Since it's made in the U.S. I knew we could get it fixed easily. So when I was ready to buy my new car, I got the basic model, but with air conditioning, because I'm going to be in that car a lot, driving from Rhode Island to visit my family in Philadelphia—and Philadelphia is the humidity capital of humidity capitals. When I get in that car, I want to be comfortable; I don't want to be sitting in a hotbox!"

To prepare for her adventure, Belinda says, "I'm going to get AAA, but this time I'm going to learn the basics. Before we had the Saturn, whenever my husband was under the car, I was in the kitchen. Now, I watch how the dealer put the spare tire on; I'm a pretty good learner. I can get right up under there; I might not get everything as tight as it should be, but I can get the tire on tightly enough to get from the road to the gas station."

Belinda wasn't always ecstatic about driving. "I never really had the urge to drive. I thought, 'What do I need a car for? I can get on the bus.' Then, all of a sudden, I thought, 'Wait a minute, I don't want to go through all this nonsense, messing with the bus schedules, rushing to finish shopping. I *need* to learn to drive, even if I do nothing but go to the hairdresser and the market. If I decide I want to go to a mall, I can go. If I'm cooking dinner, and I realize I ran out of something, or if I want to make a cake, I can get in the car. Now it takes five minutes to go to the market, and I'm home in less than twenty minutes. It's not an all-day event. Driving makes a big difference; it really does.

"My daughter Dominique got her license one day, and was on the highway up to Boston the very same day, going in the slow lane, and when she came back, she drove in the fast lane! My daughters love the idea of me driving; we've been out every night this week! I've got six weeks to practice, so I've got to drive a little bit each day, to pick up my speed, so that by the time I take my test I come out of there with my license. Then, when it comes time to do my Christmas shopping, I don't have to take anybody with me; I can get in the car and do it myself."

The Ortiz household is back to normal now that Belinda's husband is no longer her teacher. "Yesterday, when we were driving, I made up my mind to ignore him, so I drove much more comfortably!

"Anybody, I don't care what age you are, if you decide you want to drive, do it! I don't let anything affect me anymore. It just feels good to do it myself!"

Belinda Ortiz from Rhode Island with her Saturn, "Marjorie."

All of our wedding photos were of our friends in front of my father's Franklin…

Imagine driving a car with a top speed of 45 miles per hour, or maybe 50 mph if you're going down a hill. It gets nine miles per gallon, but its engine is air-cooled, and it comes equipped with a cigar lighter and lady's compact mirror in its rear seat. Imagine driving this car three hundred miles and loving every minute of it. The car is a blue 1928 Series 12B Franklin Sedan owned and cherished by Susan Roberts.

Susan is a fourth-generation Franklin owner. "The only model car my great-grandfather would own was a Franklin. He owned at least four of them. They were unusual cars, being air-cooled, and were in the same league as Cadillacs are now. My grandfather owned Franklins until he couldn't afford them any longer during the Depression, and then his brother owned Franklins, and now there's my father who owns three Franklins.

"The company began production in 1902, and continued until 1935. My great-grandfather owned one in 1908, which was pretty early for car ownership."

Susan's father owned other classics, including a Nash and a Packard, and Susan admits, "I grew up without any specific Franklin focus until I was twelve, and attended my first Franklin Trek with my parents in 1970; since then, I've participated in twenty Treks.

"The Trek is held in Cazenovia, New York, a beautiful community with a nice college, so we stay in college dorms, eat college food, share bathrooms, and we know what everybody looks like in the morning, and it's just terrific! For one week in August, up to one hundred pre-1943 air-cooled cars and their owners from all over the U.S. and Canada gather; it's like old home week."

Susan first met her husband, David, at the 1982 Trek, where her mother pushed her to "meet these nice twin boys." Susan remembers, "At the time, David had these big pork chop sideburns and this horribly shaped mustache and all I could think was 'Yech.' At the 1986 Trek, David was there. His sideburns and mustache were gone, and he was still single. I decided to just go for it!" A few years later, they married. The day before the wedding, Susan's father had his 1922 Franklin in pieces in the garage; trying to fix its clutch. "I said, Daddy, we don't *have* to drive to my wedding in your Franklin," but of course, it was fixed, and delivered them to their wedding. "Most people get photographs of the bride's family, the groom's family, and a lot of family shots, but all our photos were of our Franklin friends in front of my father's Franklin.

"While I was growing up, my father had a gas station. I was paid $2 an hour to pump gas all summer. Plus, if I filled the tonic machine, I'd get a tonic! I've been around the cars, the grease, the gasoline, and the smells all my life." Susan's office walls display photos of her car, and everyone she works with at the Emerson Majestic Theater knows about her obsession. Once the vacation schedule calendar is out, "the first thing that goes on is the Trek, because I'm taking that week off, come hell or high water! I've even dreamed of driving my car to the Trek. I wake up, and think I'm there." It's no wonder then, that when Susan married, atop the wedding cake was not the standard model of a bride and groom, but a miniature replica of Susan's automotive love, her 1928 Series 12B Franklin.

Susan Roberts from Massachusetts with her 1928 Series 12B Franklin Sedan.

We don't have churn dashes and marine compasses around us as inspiration for our quilts, but we have hubcaps…

Paula Foresman relies on the roomy contours of her "very practical" 1992 Mercury Sable to tote fabrics, rotary cutter, tool boxes, frames, cutting boards, books, and dozens of her quilts to exhibitions, classes, and quilters' conferences. "My choice of car is totally pragmatic."

Don't be misled by the utilitarian nature of Paula's relationship with her car. This Mercury wagon motivated Paula to invent her own wild wheels. Her studio showcases exquisite examples of traditional quilt design, using churn dashes, stars, flower baskets, Amish quilts, and crazy quilt motifs. But one afternoon Paula's Mercury led her to contemplate the creation of a more contemporary quilt.

"I was waiting in the car dealership while having my car fixed, glancing around. There were all these *different* cars in the showroom, and I started to think about all the design effort that goes into just one little part; the hubcap or wheel cover. I thought about traditional quilt patterns. We don't really have churn dashes and mariner's compasses around us anymore as inspiration for our quilts, but we have other objects all around us for inspiration, and one of them just might be a hubcap.

"It used to be that when women quilted, they were actually looking at the mariner's compasses. They weren't representing them exactly, the compasses were simply sources of inspiration for a circular design."

After photographing the hubcaps, Paula began interpreting nine different hubcaps into an extraordinary piece of quilt art. "Most everything on this quilt is done by machine. For a quilt to work everything has to relate to everything else. The hubcaps are designed from black, white, and gray fabrics. The fabric piecing, the patchwork, all have to relate to the quilting stitches holding the three layers of fabric together. When I was putting in the borders of this quilt, I looked at tire ads in the Sears catalog, and used the tire treads for the pattern of my quilting.

"I don't shy away from machines in any way, and I enjoy mechanical things, but I couldn't tell you which car has which hubcap. I'm not looking at the cars, I'm looking at the design of the hubcaps. My life goes into my quilts. Anything I see is a potential quilt. Machinery is powerful, and it's powerful imagery as well; it just grabs me. Everything gets related to quilts ultimately!"

Paula Foresman from Massachusetts with her hubcap quilt, inside her 1992 Mercury Sable.

All you need is a valid driver's license and a heavy foot...

At the tender age of one week, Heidi Osborne and her twin brother were nestled in their mother's arms at the track to watch her father win a race.

Her entire family has been involved in auto racing, her father for forty-five years before his death. Heidi says, "I think I was a natural at driving fast, because I was around racing all the time. Either you're going to get out there and go fast, or you're just never going to do it!"

At age seventeen, Heidi entered her first Powder Puff race. "At that time, they only held one Powder Puff race in a year. You could race in your husband's or boyfriend's car. Ron, the man who became my husband, raced with a little Volkswagen Beetle, so that Beetle was the first car I ever raced. The Powder Puff was held at the end of each racing year, only after all the husbands and boyfriends were done earning their points to win championships." Naturally, the very first Powder Puff race Heidi entered, Heidi won.

Today, women's auto racing is no longer relegated to an annual event using husbands' and boyfriends'

cars, and Heidi regularly races one of her two 1981 Volkswagen Rabbits in the men's four-cylinder class Enduro races. One Rabbit is used for her Maine races, the other for her New Hampshire races, but Heidi is quick to point out that both Rabbits are "members of the family, and they're both 'stock;' they are not modified to obtain faster speeds during the fifty- to sixty-lap Enduro races. The category I ride in, the men's four-cylinder Enduro, is non-stop racing. They don't throw yellow flags in this race. If you're crashed in the middle of the track, they don't stop the race.

"I've had my New Hampshire Rabbit for six years now; it's a factory car, but to look at it, you wouldn't say it looks great." Heidi's Rabbit isn't a car you can drive to the market; and it's not a daily driver. "It isn't street legal. Except for the windshield, there are no windows; everything has to be stripped out of it but the driver's seat. I've got a safety harness and a roll bar, but the headlights and tail-lights—everything that could fall off when you're racing—the mirrors and chrome, everything like that, has to be taken off." Heidi's helmet and fireproof suit are absolute essentials.

"The Rabbit's pretty beat up. If you see me race, you're going to understand why my car looks the way it does. To look at it, you wouldn't think it would go fast, but it does; it flies!" Sixty-five or seventy miles an hour doesn't sound that fast to highway drivers, but remember that Heidi is driving fifty to sixty laps around a small oval track.

For a little beat-up car, it sounds as if Heidi's done pretty well in her class of racing. "The races usually pay $200 to the winner. They pay down to the fifth spot, and the top five always get a trophy. I don't spend a lot. I've made money with this car, though 99 percent of the people don't make their money back, but I usually place in the top five or seven." Heidi has won up to $500 for various races, and thanks to her sponsors she's able to keep speeding along.

"Some of the racers don't have sponsors, they do it all on their own. Tony's Used Auto Parts sponsors me; they're kind of like a junkyard, so if I need struts, they supply me, and the motor came from another auto parts company, and a painting and contracting company bought my firesuit. A welding company sponsors me, and they've welded my car down at the track." Last but not least in Heidi's roster of sponsors is Brown's garage, owned by her brother. "So that's why I've made money, because I have no money in the car, and usually, whenever I finish a race, I'm in the top five!"

Being one of the top five contenders offers rewards greater than money. "Everyone knows me at the track. I get a lot of respect from men; total respect from the men, but the women racers, it's weird, some of them won't talk to me. I think it has to do with the competition."

When she's on the track, it's the adrenaline that grabs her. "Wednesday night, I raced and got knocked out early; my twin brother was out there leading the race for a long time, then he started overheating, and just to watch him I was going nuts! I couldn't stand not being on the track. My mom, who's sixty-two, used to be a Powder Puff champion; she's a spectator now, and my twin brother races, and my husband has won many a championship, but now he's my pit crew. My eight-year-old son Billy considers himself my crew chief, and I think my daughter Caitlin will get into racing too."

Twelve years ago, Heidi's brother Fred was killed while racing. "The whole family was there when he died; it was a freak accident. But we always said Fred wouldn't have wanted us to quit; it's in our blood. Not a day goes by that I don't think about my brother and my Dad. They're always out there with me when I'm racing; I talk to them all the time when I'm in the car, and I've got their numbers and names on the side of my car.

"Now when I watch other drivers, if I see somebody hit the wall, it brings tears to my eyes; it brings back everything. But to be out there racing is a whole different thing; I have no fear at all. I look at racing differently now. I would never scream out for someone to, 'Put 'em in the wall.' I would never say anything like that, because I would never want to see anybody get hurt.

"I've been in a couple of pretty good accidents. I've rolled my car over, and I've hit the wall, but the most I've ever hurt is my arm. The next day I raced again. I didn't want to tell them I was hurt, because they wouldn't have let me race, so I won that race using one arm!"

Still, Heidi knows not to take risks with her equipment. "My husband works on my car, he hasn't complained yet, and I know pretty well what's going on with my car, the noises, and when it's not handling just right.

"Any woman who likes a challenge would love this Enduro racing! Any woman who likes to drive cars fast, where there's no speed limit, who's thinking about racing, can certainly try this kind of racing. It's cheap to get into, and very popular. All you need is a valid driver's license and a heavy foot!"

Heidi Osborne from New Hampshire with one of her 1981 Volkswagen Rabbit race cars.

I decided to make my car a memorial to Grandma Ruth…

Growing up, Randi Pantera Pickett spent summer vacations with her grandparents at their home in Dallas, Texas. She fondly remembers the clinking Coke bottles in her grandmother's refrigerator, and that the refreshments were served with unconditional love.

In 1991, after completing a two-year stint in the Peace Corps teaching forestry in Mali, West Africa, Randi returned to her grandparents' doorstep. "When I came back from Africa, I didn't really have any plans; I was re-acquainting myself with my own culture. I was just hanging around, and there was my grandma Ruth's car, sitting in their driveway with nobody driving it, getting all rusted. My grandparents had tried to sell it, but these big old American cars don't sell very well. One day, my grandfather said, 'You ought to take that car.' I hemmed and hawed. It was just this *big* old 1978 Grand Prix, and I didn't think it would suit me to drive a car that was such a gas guzzler, but then I got inside, and it was *really* comfortable. When I looked at the odometer, I saw it only had 55,000 miles, and this was in 1991! So, it *was* an old car, but it didn't have many miles. It really was the little-old-lady-driving-to-church car. My grandparents gave it to me, and even now it gets sixteen miles to the gallon, which is not so bad."

For five years, Randi drove the Grand Prix as-is; a plain but comfy big car. But in 1996, her grandmother, Ruth Katherine Wallace Edwards, died at age eighty-six.

After Grandma Ruth's death, Randi began thinking of ways to celebrate her spirit. "I've always been fascinated by the Mexican and Latin American Day of the Dead celebrations. They have this idea that their ancestors come back for that day, and enjoy the things they liked when they were living, so I decided to make my car a memorial to Grandma Ruth. If my grandmother came back for a day, she'd want to play the piano, listen to Amazing Grace, drink Cokes, and she'd probably want to do a crossword puzzle and play some games.

"Most everything on the car came from yard sales and thrift stores. I used anything that was inexpensive and attractive to me. A friend was getting rid of a piece of Astroturf, so I said, 'Hey, I'll put it on the car.' I found an old guitar in the trash can, cut it in half and put it on the car, kind of like tail fins. I cut off a hank of my hair, because it was a pain to have long hair, attached it to a fishing pole and put it on the car, too, and of course there are pictures of Grandma Ruth and Coke bottles too. At one point, several years ago, I tried to sell this car, and I couldn't get anybody interested in it, and now I'm so glad."

Driving her memorial to Grandma Ruth, Randi says, "I meet people I would never meet. I really like to see people's reactions. Some people I can see hate it, because it's junk, trash. It's not organized like everything else; this car is chaos. But Grandma Ruth really loved me, and I always knew that. I would call my grandparents and tell them, 'I'm not doing very well, I don't have a big job, and I'm not this big career woman.' Grandma Ruth always used to say, 'Well, we love you, no matter what.' I never got that from anyone else in my life when I was growing up. She was a very accepting woman.

"My car is art to me, but I don't know whether it would be to anyone else. It depends how you define art. I think Grandma Ruth would probably have thought my car is silly and crazy and fun, but I know she would have liked it; she would have liked it because I did it."

Randi Pantera Pickett from Arizona with her 1978 Grand Prix, "The Grandma Ruth Car."

Driving my car is a natural high…

Linda Kaknes' car wasn't the only 1960s Ford Mustang at this particular classic car cruise night, but it was the one with the prettiest, pearliest, aqua blue paint job. Paint and polish count for quite a bit among classic car aficionados. Attention to these details lets people know you're serious about your "baby," and one thing is for sure, Linda is serious about having fun with her 1967 Ford Mustang. The first words out of her mouth are, "It's my soulmate."

Linda's affection for the Mustang dates back to the 1960s. "I had a 1966 Ford Mustang back in high school. I'd saved money since I was a kid; birthday money, piggy-bank pennies, and money from jobs, so in 1969 during my junior year I bought my first Mustang. I was on cloud nine." She just might have owned the car before she took possession of her driver's license. "I remember driving the Mustang up and down our driveway. As soon as they came out, I fell in love; I liked their shape, the horses, and I always loved the song, 'Mustang Sally.'

"My Mustang's radio was usually blasting Led Zeppelin or Jimi Hendrix, and back then, there were all kinds of hot rods; the guys had the Camaros, the Chevys, and the Crown Victorias, but my Ford Mustang was more of a 'girly' car. As soon as they came out, I knew I had to have one! But, after three years, my boyfriend told me the engine was going, and I got talked into selling it. I was young and naive, and went for the guy instead of the vehicle. What followed was a series of forgettable cars; there was even another Mustang, but it was more of a junk box than transportation."

Through marriage and motherhood, Linda drove a series of "just plain cars. But when I turned thirty, feeling old, I decided that was it! I have to have something that's mine—not his, not theirs, just mine." Linda is emphatic, "This is *my* car!

"The car was originally from South Carolina, so that meant no rust. A very dear friend of mine, Billy, came across the car, and he knew I had an eye open for one. He wanted me to get the car at a good price, and told them it was for his sister!" Linda laughs. "The thing is, as soon as the sellers saw me, they knew I wasn't his sister, since Billy's Black. I remember laughing and saying, 'Different mothers, we had different mothers!'

With 89,000 original miles on its original engine, there was only one other item the Mustang needed, a restorative paint job. Linda admits she paid more for the paint job than she originally paid for the car sixteen years ago, but knows it's worth it. "It was done completely by hand. The man who painted it took photos for his portfolio, and even made me a videotape about what he did. Most shops wouldn't want you to see what they were doing, or where there were taking short cuts!"

Still, it was traumatic. After all, Linda had to relinquish her soulmate for two and a half months. "There was one guy going up and down the whole car, looking at every bit of surface for forty-five minutes! It looked scary when he took the car apart. I felt like I was having an operation! Finally, when I went to pick it up, he must have thought I was a little touched. I mean, I just walked in the door and yelled, 'Oh my God! Oh my God! Oh my God!' at the top of my lungs. I was jumping around like a little kid I was so excited!"

It seems there are more men than women who own classic cars, although the numbers of women are increasing. "Maybe women have to get divorced first! Maybe it's because it's expensive; you know, men are used to getting under the hood, they can do this, they can do that, they pull things apart, and women aren't as secure. When you have to pay for every little thing, or heaven forbid, there's a noise under the hood, it gets very expensive for women. I don't know how many miles to the gallon I get, but I check all the fluids; it's a straight six-cylinder engine, and from being married to someone who knew cars I can tell sounds, I can say, 'It sounds like the starter.' I'm lucky. I've had the same mechanic work on it for all the sixteen years I've owned it.

"Driving my car is a natural high. I love it when the twelve- and thirteen-year-old kids just stop in their tracks and point. I know it's the car, and they're wondering, 'Who is that old lady driving that car?'"

Meanwhile, like a mother bear protecting her cub, Linda proudly stands alongside her Mustang, answering questions and accepting admiring gazes. Linda admits, "I love the cruises. It's independent and social; it gets me out of the house and I meet people.

"My Mustang is my pride and joy. This is a treasure; a jewel. It is, without a doubt, my soulmate. No guy comes close. I never plan on selling. I probably should have put the money into the house instead of the car, but I do have my priorities. At thirty, I bought the Mustang, at forty I got a tattoo, and when I turn fifty, maybe I'll get a motorcycle."

Linda Kaknes from Massachusetts with her 1967 Ford Mustang.

Women have a big attraction to cars…

Ann Harithas and her artist assistants turn steel structures into art. Working alongside artist Larry Fuentes, Ann helped create what might have been Houston's first art car. After transforming its sleek automotive exteriors, Ann was hooked. "Women have a big attraction to cars."

When Ann's brother gave her a "plain 1970-something Impala" and said, "Do something with it," Ann obeyed. "The first thing I did was to make sure the motor would run well. The big fault of most art cars is spending hundreds of hours fixing up a car that won't really run. So the first thing to do is to make sure it runs, and only then would I turn it into an art car. If you do things the other way, you're looking at trouble.

"'Swamp Mutha' is in shades of brown, swamp-like. I've got gold alligator upholstery, an alligator on the top of the car, and geese. And the skull is not a real human skull, of course, but it is real alligator on the back. I thought it really finished the car, but it added another twenty-five pounds. We haven't had any problems getting Swamp Mutha registered so far. It does go sixty miles per hour without anything falling off, and I've driven it from Houston all the way to Louisiana and back!"

Ann's next project is a "parked car" which will become a park bench. In her driveway is a 1958 Cadillac she found a few weeks ago for $3,000. Ann says, "I think it's going to be a great car. I'm not going to make an art car out of it. I'm going to keep it classic; I think it's too perfect, if you know what I mean."

Ann appreciates all cars, but especially loves older cars. "Older cars have more individuality. You'd remember each year when they'd come out it would be exciting, but they don't come out like that anymore." She yearns for the excitement of "new model season" and doesn't remember a time when she didn't drive. Ann grew up on a ranch and learned to drive her grandmother's Thunderbird at age nine or ten. "On my parent's ranch you wouldn't really hit anything. I took the parallel parking part of my driver's test right next to my grandmother's house, with my whole family watching me. I almost died, and finally they said, 'Well, never mind, you got everything else right, so you pass the test.' I got my license at fifteen. I don't remember ever NOT driving."

Ann Harithas from Texas with her Chevrolet Impala, "Swamp Mutha."

If there's anything that's preparation for being a museum director and a steam car mechanic, it's got to be a liberal arts education…

Susan Davis doesn't make any commission on the cars she "sells." No titles exchange hands, but she's more enthusiastic than any salesperson. The cars haven't been manufactured in over seventy years, but as the director of the Stanley Steamer Museum, Susan offers unbridled enthusiasm and appreciation for the creations of the Stanley family of Kingfield, Maine.

Susan understands people who start one business, and end up in another, because that's what happened to the Stanley family, and to Susan. "The Stanleys got into the car business through the back door. They were already involved in the photography business, manufacturing dry plates, and they were interested in bicycles, the recreation of the 1890s. In 1897, they built themselves a car, and were invited to demonstrate it the following year. The Stanley car performed better than the official entries, so people began saying, 'Hey, I want one of those!' and as many as one hundred orders poured in over the next two weeks.

"At the very beginning of automotive history, you could take your choice of vehicles; gas, steam,

electric, or a little bit of everything. The Steamer did very well in hill climbing, so for a while it was more popular than gasoline-powered cars. The gas cars couldn't beat the Stanleys for love nor money; the only way they could beat them was to exclude them from races. Until 1908, there were more steam cars registered in Massachusetts than gasoline-powered cars, but in 1908 Henry Ford came out with the Model T.

"People began to like the internal combustion engine better than the steam engine, because they wanted the whole engine in one package. Yet, the Stanley Steamers' performance was always fantastic at that time; they were more dependable early on than gas-powered cars. There was an awful lot about them that would have made an attractive car; except they were difficult to operate. They were not 'get in and go' cars.

"To get them running, first of all, you have to get all the liquids up to a certain level. You have to make sure you have oil, fuel, water in the boiler, and water in the storage tank. Then you have to make sure the two fuels, the pilot fuel, and the burner fuel are pressurized. Then you have to preheat the metal of the pilot in order for it to vaporize that pressurized fuel. Basically, it's very much like a gas stove with a pilot; the pilot lights the burner, the burner heats the water, the water makes steam, and then the throttle lets the steam out of the boiler and back to the engine, which makes the engine run. You need to check *all* those systems.

"You practically had to have an engineering degree to run them, but the Stanleys were bright people; they loved having these complex cars that could outperform everybody. The Stanley was marketed to women because it could be started with a match, and had no difficult crank. Steamers limped along until 1924, even though by 1915 steam cars were already dead."

But to Susan, and many others, the Stanley Steamer never really died. After all, Susan lived in Kingfield, Maine, where the Stanley family lived, and she was familiar with their automotive and business accomplishments. Susan was running a restaurant when she learned that the town planned to tear down the old Stanley School building. "Since it had already been the Stanley School, it was a natural to become the Stanley Museum." She didn't yet realize how it would transform her life. "The town fathers were upset enough, and said, 'Okay, you're going to have to figure out a way to support it.'"

Susan found allies wherever she could. "The first-ever tour of steam car owners decided to visit the birthplace of the Stanley, and we used their tour to kick off our efforts for the founding of the museum. The Stanley family was for us, so I guess that's why the museum took off like a shot. One thing led to another, and we had a museum on our hands!" She'd already saved the building from demolition, but now realized her involvement was going be more than the founder of a museum. If she was going to run this museum, she needed to become a proficient steam car mechanic as well.

"I said to myself, 'If I'm going to be connected to these steam car people, I guess I ought to know something about these things.'" Fortunately, help lived less than an hour away. "One of the museum's local advisors, Maynard Leighton, always brought a steam car whenever we needed one. He was one of the best steam car operators, so every Tuesday during the warm months he taught me, and he taught me well."

In 1985, the Stanley Museum bought its first Stanley, and Susan put her skills to the test. In 1987, the museum was given a Stanley in running condition, and today keeps another on permanent exhibit. "The three cars are early, middle, and late examples of the twenty-five years the cars were manufactured. We have a wonderful example of a horseless carriage, a 1910 coffin-nosed car, and a 1916 Stanley. I had to take them apart and put them together and make them run; I didn't have any steam car people nearby to help me, so I just learned what I needed to make them run."

As much as she credits Maynard for his automotive lessons, Susan is emphatic about the value of education. "I am a wonderful example of the importance of a liberal arts education." A graduate of Bates College, with an English degree, and minors in religion and philosophy, Susan received a master's degree from Fairleigh Dickinson University, and taught German. "In my life, I had chosen the route of language and writing, rather than doing anything mechanical, so I developed verbal skills. Being a steam engine mechanic is thinking stuff. If you have a good, basic liberal arts education, you can do anything, and if there's ever anything that's preparation for being a museum director and a steam car mechanic, it's got to be a liberal arts education.

"Knowing how to operate these cars is critical to running the museum successfully; it is, after all, a man's hobby, and still not a woman's hobby. I'm sure I would have a hard time garnering the respect of the owners, 99 percent of whom are men, if I didn't run the cars as well as I do. I'm the only person they've known as the director, and the fact that I run the cars garners tremendous respect. Even though there are a lot of women who love these cars passionately, it really is male-dominated still."

But that doesn't matter to Susan, because she's too busy raising two children, working at the restaurant, running the museum, and fielding inquiries from seven hundred worldwide members. Besides, there's always the joy of driving. "It is exhilarating to sit up high in the 1910 Stanley with all its acceleration and the wind in your face."

Susan Davis, Director of the Stanley Museum, Maine, sitting in a 1910 Stanley Steamer.

I never call it "car trouble" anymore, I call it the "car situation"…

Suzanne Faulkner acquires her inspiration and automotive attitude from a mixture of unlikely sources. Wherever she drives her greenish 1975 Dodge Dart known as "Dannygirl," she counts a gold Volkswagen Sunbug, Nancy Drew books, breakdowns, coffee cup mottoes, movies, and her father the football coach among her most important influences.

Says Suzanne, "My father was a defensive line football coach, so he's very much into technique, and I learned to drive on one of those gold, souped-up Volkswagen Sunbugs. He always taught the linemen what the proper stance was, and he treated me the same way when I was learning how to drive. He really taught me technique. I practiced parallel parking like it was going to change the world."

Suzanne also remembers the driving experiences of fictional characters. "In Nancy Drew books, she's always talking about her roadster. Nancy Drew was very much into her car, and she always drove very adroitly, very skillfully. If she needed to go fast, she did. I love Nancy Drew, she had the car, and the father who let her do what she wanted, because she never abused her privileges. That girl detective thing really had me. She's a great little heroine!"

Suzanne is also insistent on the importance of being in good physical shape. "I'm a jock chick. I was always into athletics, and for several years in North Carolina I was part of the American Dance festival. I love yoga, and I did Akido very seriously." But what's the connection between Suzanne's love of sports, martial arts, and driving?

Remember that the Dodge Dart only cost Suzanne $300 in 1988, and it is over twenty years old. "If you're going to drive a car like mine, you *have* to be in good physical shape, because quite honestly, it could break down at any moment. You could be in the middle of nowhere, and you've got to get from point A to point B, so you can't be scared to lock your stuff in the trunk and run for help.

"I've made sure I had a coin and run to the phone booth in the middle of the night. Or you can walk if you've got that kind of time. So I think there's no excuse for being out of shape physically. I'm not talking about a look, but about always having sensible shoes so that you can have a car like mine and a lifestyle like mine, and when things go wrong they never go so wrong that you can't get your own fine self out of it."

Suzanne offers her own experiences as cautionary tales. She learned her lesson just after moving to Philadelphia. "I had a rare night off, so I was driving around trying to learn the city, when I broke down. I had to walk *many* miles, since I had no money for a cab, and I didn't know the bus system. By the time I got to a gas station, I'd almost forgotten about the car trouble, it had taken me so long, and I was even calm. The guy at the gas station was drinking from a coffee cup that said, 'Poor planning on your part does not necessarily mean emergency on my part,' so that's how I think of car trouble now.

"If my fan belt breaks, and I don't have a spare fan belt in my trunk, it's nobody's problem but my own. If somebody stops to help me, or I get to my appointment on time, great! I never call it 'car trouble' anymore; I call it the 'car situation.'"

In honor of her father's old gold VW Sunbug, Suzanne spray paints her running shoes gold, and credits a movie and a guy named Tom for her decision to shake that can of gold paint onto "Dannygirl."

"I always wanted to paint 'Elvis Lives' on my car. In the movie, *Into the Night*, Michelle Pfeiffer's older brother is an Elvis impersonator who drives around in a big car that says 'The King Lives.' Michelle Pfeiffer looks so good driving around in that car. I thought the car should say 'Elvis Lives.' I thought about doing it to my car, but never did. Then this new guy showed up at work. He's an inspiring kind of guy, and I'm sure he's inspired a lot of chicks to do a lot of things!

"There was a little pocket of time at the restaurant, a lull, so we went to my car, and got the gold spray paint. My car was parked right outside the door and he whispered words of encouragement into my ear as I painted."

The relationship Suzanne shares with her Dodge Dart might soon be coming to an end. "I'm the first girl to own this car, and its license plate spelled 'DNH,' so its name is 'Dannygirl.' We've been together for over 200,000 miles. For a while, she was eating up starters, and now her flywheel's going. A friend is supposed to take me to one of those U.S. government car auctions. But I'm not doing this until Dannygirl is D-E-A-D. I don't want to start talking about her like she's going. I can't talk about other cars anywhere near my car. You can't have two cars at the same time, it's like having two boyfriends. Maybe you could in high school, but now it's too much trouble!"

Suzanne Faulkner from North Carolina with her 1975 Dodge Dart, "Dannygirl."

I paint, do ceramics, play the piano, cook and clean, and I can do fanbelts, distributor caps, spark plugs…

Laura Vannah is twenty-seven, standing at the crossroads of her life, seeing where she wants to go, learning what she can do, and discovering what she might accomplish next. She's preparing to return to her beloved Halifax, Nova Scotia, filling her 1986 Mazda 626 to the brim with her belongings and her two cats.

"You should know about the things I can do; I quilt, I sew and knit babies' and toddlers' clothes. I paint, do ceramics, play the piano, cook and clean, and I can do fanbelts. I can do distributor caps. But on the 1986 Mazda 626 I drive these days, knock on wood, nothing major has happened yet. I've done spark plugs, which cost $1.89 each. You have six of them; it's no big deal. I've done oil changes; to me, those are minor things. My major problem right now is that my carburetor is going. If my car was computerized I'd be up a creek."

Laura credits her Canadian former husband for pointing her in the right direction. "My ex-husband worked alongside Americans on a military base in Newfoundland, with a wonderful auto body shop. I really learned on my Canadian 1987 Hyundai Pony. I did *everything* on that car. I was one of two females who used to bring in our cars. Of course, this was strictly a do-it yourself shop. The guys had the mechanical expertise, and they showed us how to do things. They'd get me started, then I would take it from there. Even if you don't take classes, you can always just get the manual for your car and do the minor stuff.

"On that Pony, I learned how to fix the points in the distributor cap. You take a gap meter; it looks like a nail file; it's all to do with the size of the gap inside the distributor cap. The size of the gap is the distance the spark is jumping from one point to another. If the points aren't gapped properly, then the spark won't jump, or even if it jumps it won't reach the other side, so your car will never start. All I had to do was take off the distributor cap, keep it in a dry place (because getting water on it is a no-no), and use my gap meter. I knew to set my points at three hundredths of a millimeter larger so it would fall back to the right gauge which was .22. You just insert the gap meter into the points, figure out where it's at, and turn the screw to open it or close it, and you're set.

"I changed its rotors, pads, shoes, disc brakes, and I knew how to replace my starter wire. I'd pop the hood and fiddle around underneath, and reconnect wires. Guys would come up, seeing a 'damsel in distress.' They asked if I needed help. 'No,' I'd say, 'That's quite all right, I know what's wrong,' and in their macho guy voice, they'd say, 'Well, we'll just stand here and make sure!' I get out my duct tape, reconnect wires, and go on my way. Duct tape is a wonderful invention!"

Pantyhose is another extraordinary invention, but not for fashion purposes. Keep it in its proper place; the trunk. "Pantyhose, tied together tightly enough, can be used like a rubber band to temporarily replace an alternator belt. The belt is what makes the alternator turn, which then powers your engine. If you don't have an alternator your engine isn't going anywhere!"

Laura is considering a career as a mechanic. "I like to do things with my hands. I love crafts, I love creating things, fixing things. When I was fixing the Pony I wanted to yell out, 'Hey; look, my car's running because of me!' I know that feeling, when you actually do something; it's wonderful."

Laura Vannah from Massachusetts with her 1986 Mazda 626.

In an electric car, there's nothing holding you back...

"When you drive an electric car, you turn the key, and nothing happens," says Janice Dauphinais. "I mean, the little red lights come on, and your fasten seat belt light comes on, and the car actually *is* on, but you don't hear anything. You select which direction you want, forward or reverse, and then you step on the accelerator (what used to be called the gas pedal), and the car starts to move, very, very quietly. As you get on the highway, you might hear a little hum from the electronic control box. It's just like cruising! You don't turn the radio up anywhere near as loud as you need to in a gas-powered car, because you're not hearing it over the din of the engine."

Janice, who claims she doesn't care that much about what she drives, spends her days caring for a fleet of twenty electric vehicles. "My job title is 'Service Coordinator and Electric Vehicle Technician' for Solectria, an electric car conversion and manufacturing company in Massachusetts. In other words, I'm a mechanic."

Becoming any kind of mechanic was the furthest thing from her mind over twenty years ago, when her first car—a 1965 Ford Comet—broke down. Janice was an art major running a natural foods restaurant. "My friends lent me tools, and I just went at it and tinkered. I didn't think this was what I was going to do when I grew up. I didn't do this when I was a kid, like most boys do, but I was really interested in how things are put together. When I started working on cars I really liked the work, even though I learned a lot of things the hard way!"

Eventually, Janice learned so much that the backyard garage she ran became a real business. She opened Stonybrook Automotive in 1988, working on gasoline-powered cars. "I don't think I experienced much in the way of prejudice. On the contrary, women would come in and say, 'I want her to fix my car; I can trust her.' My partner, a guy, would go nuts—it was prejudice in reverse. We had different fortes anyway. I'd fixed cars in the same area for twelve years, I had a following, and my partner had a following, so between two followings we had a business!

"By 1994, cars were getting more complicated. A general repair shop like ours would either have to hone in on specific cars, or tool up for every make. I thought about moving on, maybe giving up cars altogether." The solution arrived one day in her electric bill, in the form of an article on electric cars. After getting a closer look at a Geo Metro converted by a company called Solectria at a local exhibit, Janice was hooked. "I opened the hood of the Metro, saw how simple it looked, and thought 'Aha. I'm going to learn about these.'"

After Selectria told her they didn't give tours, Janice contacted several universities' solar car projects and struck pay dirt. "The Massachusetts Institute of Technology (MIT) faculty adviser, a woman my age said, 'Come on over. We work Monday nights and all day Saturdays. You can help us weigh up fiberglass.' So I did the messy work for quite a while, learned quite a bit, mostly about teamwork, what it takes to build a car, and a bit about batteries. It takes a lot of grunt work, engineering, and thinking about things. You consider every little ounce and gram of what you're putting on the car, and you make it count, so you can make the car very, very slippery as the wind sees it. Aerodynamics are extremely important, which is why all the cars are starting to look alike these days. If you can make a car lighter or faster it takes less energy to move it down the road.

"I have to figure out how much energy something is using, so I'll fall back on high school math and algebra. Energy equals current times resistance. I use it everyday."

These days, Janice's job at Solectria is to keep the electric vehicles owned or leased by the state of Massachusetts running, but her first priority is dealing with customer calls. "Hopefully, I have a mechanic on the other end, somebody who can use a voltmeter, and I walk through a diagnosis. There aren't a lot of calls, but there's a lot of follow up. We either fix the cars here, or dispatch them to a local garage. Someone might call up saying, 'My brake feels spongy.' I need to decide whether I should see the car because it's an EV problem, or the corner gas station can see the car because it's a brake problem.

"I write manuals, work on upgrade kits, help the Engineering Research and Development department, and if something needs driving, I'll test-drive." Though she doesn't have an EV of her own, she regularly gets to test drive EVs to her home about twenty miles away. "Since I can recharge them in any old plug, it means I can live on the third floor and throw the extension cord out the window."

Janice's favorite driving music is the hum of the EV; she never even turns on the radio. "I like to listen to the hum. Basically, my job is to listen for noises, or any possible problems, so I like to cruise along. When you lift your foot off the accelerator, you can be in 'regenerative' mode, where regenerative braking begins, and the car starts to slow without having to step on the brakes. You can also switch into coast where the car does exactly that. In an EV there's nothing holding you back."

Half the miles driven in the world, according to Janice, are driven in the United States. "It is going to be a long time before Americans give up their individual cars, if ever. But even though we can't harvest oil, we *can* generate electricity."

Technology is changing, and so is the mechanic's job. "Being a mechanic is getting to be more of a white coat job. I think it takes a very intuitive, caring person to be a good mechanic. If women have an edge at all, it's because they tend to be caring." Janice offers some advice: "Don't be afraid to open up the hood and look around. Read your owner's manual—it has some very good information."

If mechanical prowess is what you're after, Janice offers advice based on what she didn't do. "I'd encourage people to go to school if they want to do things the right way, and to pay attention in algebra class. Plumbers still do better than mechanics, so if you're in it for the money, I'd say go be a plumber! But if this wasn't fun for me, I wouldn't be here. This is fun because I never know what they're going to hit me with, or what's going to be on my chair in the morning, or what problem I have to unravel.

"One of my biggest stumbling blocks, my whole life, is thinking I can't do something, and even here, it comes up again and again. They'll send me off, saying 'Go down there and deal with this car,' and I'll say to myself, 'But I don't know about this; blah, blah, blah.' In the back of my head there is still that little voice that says 'You don't have enough experience; what if it doesn't work?' Well, then you fix it because you have to and you need to get where you're going. That's what a car is for me; it's not about performance and horsepower, which it more often is for men; for women it's about going where we want to go."

Janice Dauphinais from Massachusetts with one of the Solectria electric vehicles that she services.

I've worked in every bookstore on the face of the earth, it seems, so covering the car with books was one of those freeform things…

If you ever find yourself wandering the roads of Houston, looking for a good book to read, you might be lucky enough to spot the Bookmobile and its owner, book seller and book lover, Andrea Foster.

Out of automotive misfortune, came automotive creation. A little more than a year ago, Andrea's beloved pickup truck was stolen. But all was not lost. Friends did what they could to comfort her. "My 1974 Pinto was given to me by a friend from Brentano's bookstore, so here I was with this 1974 Pinto which is great; I've been driving it around ever since. I've worked in every bookstore on the face of the earth it seems; so covering the car with books was one of those freeform things."

Five of Andrea's bookstore friends leapt to the challenge. "We knew we wanted to do it, and that we had the books to do it, so we just went at it, and the car kind of developed itself." She never imagined herself driving an art car. "I'm not the new car type, and I've always liked pickup trucks, but this car is my everyday car."

There's no specific genre of reading material on the Pinto. Andrea just likes the idea of encouraging

reading. The Pinto is an ever changing library. Ever vigilant about the possibility of books flying off the Pinto at highway speeds, Andrea claims to know every surface road route in Houston. "I always keep a glue gun in the back seat. Used books can be cheap and I'm always reading. More than being attached to any one place at which I've worked, I'm attached to books. There are always more books!"

Andrea Foster from Texas with her 1974 Pinto, "Bookmobile."

I'd been in accidents, so this all started because I wanted people to see me…

Today Carter Ernst, who teaches sculpture at the University of Houston, has two decorated daily drivers, "Kitsch Cargo," a 1984 Mazda, and "Blind Vision," a 1980 Toyota truck she only recently completed, and considers temporary. "I bought the truck from my Dad as security for when Kitsch Cargo, with its 209,000 miles, breaks down, because I knew it would be good art car material. I hadn't done anything to it until this week, but now that it's started being an art car there's no turning back."

Carter's original automotive ambitions weren't solely artistic. They were born out of a desire for safety and survival on the streets of Houston. "I'd been in accidents, so this all started because I wanted people to see me. I had a small grayish blue Honda that just blended in; this was before all the cars started getting smaller; you could hardly see it. I was concerned about safety, so as part of a collaboration with other artists, I started putting glass, mosaic, and a variety of items on this Datsun 210, known as the Oozemobile.

"When I turned the Datsun into an art car, my mother was pretty mad at me. She couldn't believe I would drive around in a car like that. Of course, I only paid $500 for it, and I drove it five years. It just kept getting better and better for those five years, until it needed too many repairs. The Oozemobile no longer rolled. About the same time I bought the car, I got my dog, Rover; she's *real* attached to the car. We were going to have it hauled off, but Rover jumped in the car, and wouldn't get out. So I thought, 'Okay, we'll just roll the windows down, and use it as a doghouse.'"

Now Kitsch Cargo is the Oozemobile's heir apparent. "Its engine is still running well, so it's just all these little things that keep happening and cost a lot. I was fretting over whether I should sink the money into it, and then my truck had problems, but in the end I decided to fix both. I couldn't really junk it and I don't want to turn it into a doghouse yet; it's too personal to me. People give me things, and there are personal mementos I don't want to scrap.

"I knew my Toyota truck would be good art car material, though it was kind of nice having a plain vehicle for a while.

"I think everybody has a relationship with their cars. Cars are a form of expressing yourself and your personality. Art cars are just more extreme—they're symbols. You may not be able to have a fancy sports car, but you can have an art car pretty easily. You just start with a hood ornament, and it grows from there."

Carter Ernst from Texas with her 1984 Mazda, "Kitsch Cargo."

Anybody can do it...

You might see twenty-six-year-old Tina Gramann's 1976 Oldsmobile Cutlass Supreme as a natural extension of her work. Five days a week, pre-school teacher Tina plays with a dozen young children. "It's a lot of fun; I just go to work and play."

This car was purchased to be decorated, as well as driven. The search was frustrating for Tina and her husband, Trey. "At first, I was going to find someone who'd want to give me a car. I made lots of calls, looked in the newspapers, and had no luck. I searched the used car lots, and tested a few clunkers and this was the first car that was working. I paid $300. It seemed to run just fine.

"A friend's kids helped paint the flower pots on the car and rode with me in our first Houston's Art Car parade. My three-year-old son, Van, loves everything about the car; he remembered last year's parade and knew we were getting ready for another parade. He likes to walk around the car and see Mommy and Daddy working on it. Van's contribution to the car is the green grass, and waving at people while I'm driving."

The second year the Oldsmobile participated in Houston's Art Car parade was its debut appearance as a convertible. Tina admits it was originally her husband's idea to cut the top off the car. "The more I thought about it, the better and better it sounded. He seemed to think a saw would work just fine, and it did!"

Despite its mechanical frailties, and the fact that it doesn't go much over 40 miles per hour, Tina says, "As a convertible, the whole car is so easygoing. It's bright and colorful, with my favorite colors, pink, yellow, and sky blue. I love being in the convertible, waving to people until I get a response. I drive it to the pre-school, and let the children look, and have them climb in and out and explore.

"When I decided to paint this car with flowers, Trey's initial reaction was to roll his eyes, but I know that deep inside it's fine with him, and he really likes it. I was never scared to begin painting it, just excited." Tina admits to always being "artsy-crafty," and advises potential car painters, "anybody with any interest, desire, or imagination can do it!"

Tina Gramann from Texas with her 1976 Oldsmobile Cutlass Supreme, "How Does Your Garden Go?"

The patina of rust is wonderful for sculpture,
but not for a vehicle you actually want to drive...

Alys Myers originally sought fame and fortune in the film industry mecca of Los Angeles. "In between sporadic film production jobs, I wanted to make sure I didn't fall into the rut of the unemployed, so I woke up early in the morning to go walking. I would pick up pieces of cars that had fallen by the side of the road, bring them home and make little sculptures with them. Eventually, I took welding classes at Otis Parsons, and the rest is history!"

Today, "Steel Structures" sculptor Alys transforms antique transmission gears, drill bits, and automotive computer parts into decorative screens, tables, chairs, and artwork in a Boston studio.

One of her favorite haunts is the junkyard. "The junkyard I go to is over one hundred years old, so I find really cool old car parts. Some days are good, some days are bad, and I don't find anything. Everything's completely different each time I go. They have piles of metals: aluminum, cast iron, steel. They smash it up into these little boxes, so everything gets wiped out, and each day it starts all over again.

"Some of the pieces I used in my decorative screen are among the very first pieces I found at the junkyard. Some of their steel piles had been leveled to where the really interesting old stuff was, and I found some great old gears. On the screen, I have three different transmission gears, bike chains, miscellaneous transmission parts, and gears, lots of gears. I love transmission gears, and the boards that sit in the transmission's computer."

As her precious cargo grew larger and larger, Alys decided she needed something larger than her much-beloved Volkswagen Jetta to transport her work between her studio and galleries.

The moment Alys began her automotive search for the Jetta's replacement, her art clashed with her needs. "I wanted an old-style Toyota Land Cruiser, and I was actually looking for two years. The new ones are bubbly shaped, and I don't like them. It takes me a very long time to buy *anything*. I do a lot of research. I looked at quite a few Land Cruisers in the area, but most all of them were rusty, especially in the back end. Rust is usually my friend. I want its funky colors and patina in my work. The patina of rust is wonderful for sculpture, but not for a vehicle you actually want to drive.

"I went through a lot of ups and downs. There were a lot of false starts." Eventually, through extensive study of the want-ads, Alys found her "Joey," a beige 1987 Toyota Land Cruiser. "Its name may be a bit farfetched, but it's kangaroo colored, and I think of it as an Australian outback vehicle. Since Joey is the Australian name for kangaroo, that's how my Joey got its name.

"The previous owner obviously kept it in good shape. I took it to a mechanic first though; I'm pretty thorough with stuff like that. I invest not only my money but my emotions. If you get even remotely attached to your vehicle, as I do, you want to make sure it is going to be around for awhile. Still, I couldn't bear to let the Jetta out of the family; so I sold it to my brother."

Alys is far too attached to consider ever selling Joey, but understands people's desire. "People come up to me all the time on the street trying to buy Joey. A guy once offered me $15,000 for it on the spot, because it was in such good shape, but each time my answer is 'No, I'm too attached!'

"The Land Cruiser is huge, but we have good parking karma. I don't always have good traffic karma, but my parking karma is quite good. I inherited it from my Dad; he's one of those guys who gets a spot right in front of the mall at Christmas, and I inherited it, just as my little brothers did. My mom doesn't have it. She's only in the family by marriage, you see. It's genetic I think, like a particular hair color or eye color."

Alys Myers from Massachusetts with her 1987 Toyota Land Cruiser, "Joey," and one of her sculptures made from gears and transmissions parts.

My whole purpose in life was always to travel the roads...

For as long as she could remember, the only job Betty Hamilton really wanted was that of a bus driver. But it turned out to be one of those occupational dreams that was tough to turn into reality. "I always, always wanted a driving job, but I was never old enough."

Betty held factory jobs until she reached the magic age of twenty-one. "I went to one of those driving schools where they teach you to drive *anything*. I never wanted to go to college; I just wanted to drive. I wanted to drive a truck, but for most of those jobs you have to be twenty-one. So as soon as I turned twenty-one I started calling courier and delivery companies, thinking I could be out on the open road."

Betty didn't get her dream job right away, but she was driving—a school bus. This job proved to be one big learning experience. "The seven-year-olds are absolutely the worst. I don't know how I managed those years as a bus driver." Finally, after a stint training new drivers, it was time for a vacation.

Most vacationers relax and see the sights. But when Betty traveled to New Mexico with her father, instead of lounging around a pool, Betty found a bus factory. "So I moved to New Mexico. That's when people began to think I was crazy; delivering buses all over the country." But after living in Roswell, New Mexico, for more than a year, Betty, a native Ohioan, decided it was time to move on.

A stint driving commuter buses through the traffic jams of Los Angeles caused Betty to yearn for the open road once again. She touched down briefly back home in Ohio then went to Nashville, hoping to drive musicians' tour buses.

Armed with plenty of professional driving experience, Betty admits, "I thought I could easily find a job, but I couldn't have been more wrong." Never one to get discouraged, Betty shifted her focus back to Ohio. "So there I was in Nashville, yet I started delivering buses out of Ohio. It was over four hundred miles from Nashville to the bus factory one way. I'd drive to the factory, pick up the bus, take it to California, or wherever it was going, and then drive back. I ended up staying in Ohio, not in Nashville."

Betty's dreams of Nashville never died. "I'd go back to Nashville, and hand the companies my resume. They'd tell me, 'Oh no, you have to be driving for years to drive for a singer. They were handing me a line; they didn't want to hire me because I'm a woman. Finally, one of the ladies who worked at a bus leasing company called me, so I ended up driving for Crystal Gayle!"

But a once-in-a-lifetime chance to tour America drew Betty away from her aspirations in the music business. The steady paycheck from a musicians' tour bus could not compete with the lure of spending eighty-four days at the wheel of the "Majic Bus," a wildly painted, eighteen-wheel bus fueled by natural gas, along with Professor Doug Brinkley and thirty college students on a cross-country college course.

"Instead of working out of a textbook, this professor takes the kids to see places and meet people all across the country, so it's a classroom on wheels." Even though the pay was good, and she wouldn't have missed it for anything, Betty admits, "The first two weeks were absolutely miserable; everybody was ready to quit!" With a classroom as big as the country, and so much on the agenda, it's no wonder, Betty claims, "It was the most disorganized thing I'd ever seen! Driving in those big Eastern cities is no fun for a bus driver; it's one big headache."

Betty and one other driver alternated behind the wheel, covering great amounts of territory. "We visited thirty-six or thirty-seven states in eighty days. We actually slept on the floor of the Civil Rights Museum, then went on to Mississippi and Alabama. If the campground was closed, we pulled up anyway. Then it was on to Georgia, where we helped build a Habitat for Humanity house with Jimmy Carter."

Despite the difficulties involved keeping several dozen roaming students and one professor ready to roll, combined with late nights, and early mornings, Betty found relief. "Once we started heading west, seeing South Dakota, North Dakota, and places like Montana, I was really surprised." Betty was awed by Mt. Zion National Park, and very happily surprised by Seattle and Mt. Rainier.

"Wherever we went, we had crowds gathering, wondering, 'What is that, a bunch of hippies?'" The nation's newspapers and media documented their travels. "When the *Today* show filmed us, they even filmed me driving the bus. Even though we couldn't write down our destination half the time, and the rest of the time we'd never get there, it was really like a paid vacation for me."

Though her future assignments may not gather media attention, the "Majic Bus" trip convinced Betty that she has chosen the right career. Besides, it whetted her appetite for travel. "I'd like to take a trip around the whole country. I've only missed about four states, but I'd like to go through *every* state. You *have* to get off the interstate to see the scenery."

Betty Hamilton from Ohio, driver of the "Majic Bus." Betty holds valid school bus,
chauffeur's, and commercial driver's licenses.

I just like to get out and see what's going on in the world...

While leafing through an adult education brochure, a painting class caught Carol Urich's attention. It involved no watercolors or easels—it was an auto painting class. One course led to another, and Carol soon found herself immersed in a series of auto mechanics classes. The more she learned, the more she grew to love her seventeen-foot 1970 Chevrolet Impala, which had once belonged to her mother.

By the time Carol was diagnosed with Multiple Sclerosis several years later, she also owned an RV. Armed with her knowledge of auto mechanics, she decided to trade in her civilian job with the military and her Washington, D.C., apartment for a trek out west to Arizona, where she could live in an RV park for women, and begin a new life.

"I really didn't want to give up my car. It cost $795 to have it shipped, tax included, so I thought I would do that, and take my time seeing the country. I took two weeks to get out here, driving the RV.

"Wherever I could, I traveled along Route 66, and then I drove in through Flagstaff. Looking at the map, I figured it would take me six hours from Flagstaff, but because my RV was so loaded up, it took twelve. There were 5 or 6 percent grades, so I'd get off at every single exit to slow down; I'd get off the exit ramp, then get right back on the entrance ramp. Normally, I get nine or ten miles a gallon, then I was getting five or six."

Two weeks later, Carol arrived at her new home, but it was four weeks until her car arrived. "I was sick without my car. For two weeks last year, when my engine was being rebuilt, I was miserable. This time, I did volunteer office work at the center here, two to four hours a day, but I told them, 'Things are going to be different when I get my car.'

"My mechanic back in Maryland had told me to drive my car as if I were angry with it, in order to burn out that carbon. This car was built when speed limits were 70 miles per hour, so when it's doing 55, it resents it. With the money from the money tree at my going away party, I bought a radar detector. My car arrived on a Friday night. I took off at 6:30 on Saturday morning and didn't come back until 6:30 that night.

"When I got back, people were asking me, 'What the hell happened to you?' 'What are you talking about?' I asked, 'it's only 6:30.' There was a whole line of people and messages. I had told them that when my car arrived I was going to be out in the world, spending time on the road! I had driven to Phoenix, stopped at yard sales, gone to a Multiple Sclerosis Society chapter meeting. I just had a really good time!"

These worriers were talking to a woman who'd once spent two and one-half months driving fifteen thousand miles around Canada, Nova Scotia, and Alaska. "I'd like to do that trip again sometime. I want to keep driving my car as long as I possibly can. To me, a car is a necessity. I just like to get out and see what's going on in the world, you know."

Carol Urich from Arizona with her 1970 Chevrolet Impala four-door sedan.

Even when I was a little kid in elementary school I loved cars…

Says Laurel Blanchard, "I used to make car models out of pencil erasers the way I saw the guys do. You'd use pins to make an antenna, thumbtacks to make the wheels, then you'd mark them up all over with magic markers, and they'd look *real* cool."

For Laurel, cars are a visual thrill. "Looks are everything. In high school during the 1970s, everybody souped up the cars. They'd tint the windows and jack the rear, and put tires on the back of the car. Women didn't soup up their cars then; only guys did. I was always wishing that I could have a souped-up car. Instead, I drove a hand-me-down 1965 Dodge Coronet; it was hideous, but it moved."

Eventually, Laurel acquired a car that remains significant in her personal automotive history: a 1976 Dodge with a slant six engine. "The slant six engine is the engine that never dies; it's like a sewing machine that keeps running. They all sound alike; you can hear them going down the street with your eyes closed, and know it's a slant six engine.

"As soon as I drove off the showroom floor I traded in the hubcaps that came with the car and bought

new wire granny hubcaps. Then I drove home, put on the pinstripes and the tinted windows. I hadn't even had the car two hours when I did that stuff. It cost about $5 a roll and took a couple of hours to tint the windows. I made sure to do it right and squeeze out the bubbles."

As the drummer for the band Lillith, Laurel recorded an album in 1976, and was paid $200. "It was time to buy mag wheels for my Dodge!

"A lot of guys made fun of me when I bought all this stuff, the wheels and everything. It costs extra money to have white tires, and it costs a lot to have chrome rims, but look at it. Back in the 1970s, they all put them on their cars. You can go to the store, buy the stuff, and just do it!

"I'm not going to pay for a vanity license plate; I won't go that far, but I had to put my imprint on my car."

Laurel Blanchard from Massachusetts with her souped-up 1976 Dodge.

My car celebrates homemakers, but not just women, because of course, men can be homemakers, too…

"Recipe of the Month" cards, pictures of food, and Tupperware. These items were not on Belinda's mind when she and her mechanic husband, Ken, attended an auto auction a few years ago. What Belinda really wanted was a "parts car" with a good strong engine, something compatible that would rescue her beloved 1963 Mercury Comet.

"Even as a kid, I loved my grandfather's Comet; its details; and its fins. I always told him, 'When you want to get rid of that car, *please* look to me, don't sell it.' When he bought himself a new car, he called and told me to pick up my car. But a week later, there was a problem. Five or six male cousins wanted the Comet. Rather than getting into a family argument, I told him to give the car to one of the cousins. Grandpa said, 'Belinda, you come and pick up your car!' It was a gift for being unselfish! I drove that Comet for a year and half, before it threw a rod and cracked the block."

The solution to Belinda's mechanical dilemma appeared in the form of a Ford Fairlane; after all; its engine was sound, and compatible with the Comet. But before the engines could be switched, Belinda got sidetracked by a large bag at a white elephant sale. "Inside the bag were all of these little children's dishes, and since I'm a pre-school teacher, and it was only fifty cents, I grabbed it." Hidden treasure was lurking at the bottom of the bag. "There were all these Tupperware giveaway items. 'This is wild,' I said to myself; 'it's the makings of an art car!'

"I didn't go out to buy an art car, but it just kind of fell together. I started thinking of recipes, big pictures of food, and Tupperware, of course. Tupperware represented the 1950s and 1960s; it reminds me of homemakers, and brings me back to childhood." The Ford Fairlane needed more Tupperware, so Belinda headed to thrift stores. "People began getting the idea I was returning the Tupperware to the distributor; apparently Tupperware has a lifetime warranty. If it's cracked or faded, you can just return it and get new Tupperware. The thrift store Tupperware pickings were downright slim, so despite the thrill of finding a stack of Betty Crocker "Recipe of the Month" cards, Belinda knew she had to look elsewhere.

With Houston's annual art car parade on the horizon, Belinda's car still needed some finishing touches. So Belinda placed a phone call to Houston's Tupperware distributor. "I wanted to see if they would consider sponsoring my car, and Ed, my contact at Tupperware, told me, 'Come on down!'

I imagined getting used, broken Tupperware from a shabby little warehouse, but even the warehouse was big and beautiful. Here was the Tupperware of the 1990s, all bright pinks, purples, and greens."

Ed was willing to give Belinda whatever she needed, but Belinda felt a part of her mission was the recycling, so she sifted through the returned pieces slated for the chipper. Ed hadn't even seen her car yet, and when he did, "His eyes popped out of his head. He brought his wife and daughter, and they must have walked around the car at least ten times. He kept saying, 'I had no idea!' Once he saw the car, he told me 'I really want to bring you more new Tupperware.'

"As I worked on Tuppertime, people would walk by and pick up the rotary phone, talk, hang up, giggle a bit, and walk on by." Since the phone came from Belinda's kitchen, you might say she's brought her kitchen on the road.

"The kitchen is the room where people hang out. I like to think the kitchen is the most beautiful room in our house. I kept thinking back to my Mom's Tupperware parties, and all the Tupperware in our house. It reminds me of homemakers; my Mom was a homemaker, and Elizabeth Montgomery on *Bewitched* was a homemaker, and I kept thinking of all the television programs of that era.

"Tupperware was a big part of my childhood. You had to have the bowls with the lids, and of course, your salt and pepper shakers were Tupperware. All the women in our neighborhood were stay-at-home moms; there were lots of kids, and when we'd go over to their houses, there was Tupperware. My car 'Tuppertime' celebrates homemakers, but not just women, because of course, men can be homemakers, too."

Belinda's Comet is still safely in storage, waiting for another engine, but Tuppertime is complete. "An art car evolves every day; you get different ideas. Whatever you put on your car people are going to touch; they're going to take things and pull, and wonder how something's stuck on. You know you're going to lose things whatever you do. When you start, you might feel insecure; that it's not as good as everybody else's, but it's part of you; so just quit thinking and do it. As soon as you start settling for something, you're compromising yourself, so get what you want, no matter how long it takes."

Belinda Crimmins from Texas with her Ford Fairlane, "Tuppertime."

I think every girl's dream growing up is to own a red convertible...

"I think every girl's dream, growing up, is to own a red convertible." Pat Boyer is living that dream. "I don't name it, but it's my baby. Even if somebody offered me a whole lot of money for it, say $10,000, I wouldn't take it; because I couldn't part with it. My husband Bill, on the other hand, says he would grab the money and take a taxicab home!

"I'd seen a picture of this Comet Caliente in a magazine, and there was a dealer in the next town. I bought my Comet brand new in 1964, for $2,500, which was a lot of money. We'd been married about eleven years, and we had four children, so I needed a car to haul the kids around in like a taxi. It was a hard thing to buy, because it was so much money. My husband said, 'You're going to have to support that car if you want it.' I could have it as long as I paid for the gas, insurance, and upkeep. The first job I had to support the car was working at a nursing home two nights a week from 3:00 to 11:00 P.M., so that's how the payments were made."

Pat not only supported the car but received a bonus: an automotive education. "The first time I knew there was something wrong with the car, the mechanic said 'I don't think your rocker arm is getting the oil.' Since that is an expensive job, I told him I'd think about it. I drove immediately from the gas station to the library, and got a manual for the Comet. I brought the manual home, and thought, 'Well, that isn't too complicated to reach.' So I took the cover off the manifold, and got down into this thing, removed it, and cleaned it all up. So I did that, and it was so satisfying, and the car ran perfectly.

"The next thing I knew there was a noise in the engine, so I took it to another garage. The mechanic told me one of the pistons was gone. Again, I drove to the library, and this time I got three books, because now I've got a whole engine to work on. I wanted to see if I could do it.

"After looking at the books, I visited one of my girlfriends, whose husband loves to tinker with cars. He offered to help me work on my car and he even let me keep my car in his garage.

"He made sure I was the one doing the work. He told me what parts to remove, and made me label and number everything that came off the car. He'd have me really clean the parts up, then I'd take them to the local auto parts shop to see whether they were okay or needed to be replaced. Eventually, I took the whole engine down to nothing. I even dismantled a car in the middle of a junkyard to get a new radiator. At that time, I worked at City Hall, and everybody knew I was working on my car, so all these men would stop by with little hints. I'd put them in the back of my head, and just go from there.

"My husband is just delighted that he can turn the key, and the engine is there, he doesn't want to know any more than that. He knows me though, and that I always have to try something at least once. So that's what I did, and now I just keep it up, and have fun.

"The Comet is definitely not a kid's car, but I figured I probably wouldn't get another car, so I better have what I want. The kids are all grown now, but when they were teenagers, they *all* wanted to borrow the car. But, I didn't weaken, they could not drive my car. That's all there was to it, and I think that's probably why I still have it!

"There was a point when people began asking me when I was going to get a new car. I didn't particularly want a new car. You do build up a relationship with a car. I like my car; it's just a matter of putting some money into it every year to keep it going. There's only 92,000 miles on it, and I drive it everyday, so I figure it's gone about three thousand miles a year. I wouldn't push my baby on the freeway to 70 miles per hour, 55 is fine. It can go faster, I just don't *want* to drive it faster. It doesn't have power steering either, so when you're driving, you *really* know you're driving.

"Not everybody has a relationship with their car, but a lot of people really like older cars. I enjoy going to the car shows, talking with people, and looking for parts." This year, Pat even received an automotive Christmas present. "My husband got a big box, and put a picture of a convertible top inside, along with my appointment to get the new top, and wrapped the box up. It was a great gift!"

Pat confides one of the secrets of her successful automotive relationship: she talks to her car. "I'll say, 'That's a good girl.' I praise my car; it's like my knitting shop. When I come into my shop I always say good morning. If I talk to my shop, I might as well talk to my car.

"Kids will stop by and see the Comet parked in front of the shop and say, 'Your car is wicked awesome!'" It's not only the kids who are fascinated by Pat and her Comet. "One day I was stopped at a red light where there were all these construction fellows standing around, and the next thing I know, they're all walking around my car. One of them said, 'Boy they don't make them like they used to!' I can't believe I was so fresh, and asked, 'Do you mean me, or my car?' and he said '*Both!*'"

Pat Boyer from Massachusettts with her bright red 1964 Comet Caliente convertible.

About the author

Marilyn Root is a professional photographer who grew up attending classic car shows with her parents. She attends the Houston Art Car Show annually, drives a 1995 Saturn decorated on the inside with mementos from her road trips, and lives in the Boston area. Her photography has appeared in newspapers, books, and magazines, as well as museum shows.